D0855868

Victorian
Parlor Games

Also by PATRICK BEAVER

The Big Ship
The Crystal Palace
A History of Lighthouses
A History of Tunnels

Victo
Parlor

793
B386

B+T 4-2-79 3¥.66

126H

FOR

JOHN BRUNEL

rian
Games

Patrick Beaver

THOMAS NELSON INC., PUBLISHERS
NASHVILLE   NEW YORK

DIXON PUBLIC
LIBRARY
DIXON, ILLINOIS

No character in this book is intended to represent any actual person; all the incidents of the story are entirely fictional in nature.

Copyright © 1974 by Patrick Beaver

All rights reserved under International and Pan-American Conventions. Published by Thomas Nelson Inc., Publishers, Nashville, Tennessee. Manufactured in the United States of America.

First U.S. edition

Library of Congress Cataloging in Publication Data

Beaver, Patrick.
  Victorian parlor games.

  Reprint of the ed. published by P. Davies, London under title: Victorian parlour games for today.
  Includes index.
  1. Indoor games.   2. Amusements—Great Britain.
I. Title.
GV1471.B36   1978   793   78–12396
ISBN 0–8407–6608–4

Contents

Eager and never weary we pursued
Our home amusements by the warm peat-fire
At evening; when with pencil and with slate,
In square divisions parcell'd out, and all
With crosses and with cyphers scribbled o'er,
We schemed and puzzled, head opposed to head
In strife too humble to be named in Verse.
Or round the naked table, snow-white deal,
Cherry or maple, sate in close array,
And to the combat, Loo or Whist, led on.

WILLIAM WORDSWORTH
THE PRELUDE, BOOK 1

Victorian Parlor Games

Satirical drawing of animals playing
a board game (Egyptian New Kingdom,
c. 3000 B.C., British Museum)

Introduction

ll games, from the Roman gladiatorial battles to a quiet round of cards or charades, are imitations of real-life situations. This is equally true of physical or mental contests, games of chance or combinations of any of these. Team games, whether played in field or parlor, are all essentially exercises in combat. Games in which the individual pits his wits against other individuals are only a reflection of the struggle to live and better oneself in the world of reality. The activity of playing games is the expression of an instinct, for play is far older than culture, older even than prehistory. In his book, *Homo Ludens (Man the Game Player)*, famed Dutch historian Johan Huizinga reminds us that animals did not wait for man to teach them their playing.

13

Animals play, but, of course, they do not "play games" for the term "play" is, technically applicable only to informal play activities: playing "cowboys and Indians," playing "hospitals," playing with dolls and toys, playing in the sand. In this form of spontaneous play there are no rules and no fixed procedure.

A *game*, on the other hand, be it Blind Man's Buff, chess, or polo, is subject to definite rules and procedures (the infringement of which usually involves a penalty of some form), and the action of the game leads to a given climax—victory for one side or person over the others.

Some indoor games of the ancient world were, like bridge and chess today, taken very seriously indeed. The Greek game of Cottabus had not only its professional players but also special buildings in which to accommodate players and spectators. The object of the game (which was inextricably linked with wine-drinking) was for the player to cast a portion of the wine left in his cup in such a way that, without breaking its bulk during its passage through the air, it should strike a special target and, by its impact, produce a distinct noise.

Unhappily Cottabus is now extinct as a common game, although English writers G. K. Chesterton and Maurice Baring used to indulge in private wine-throwing battles between themselves. Only port wine was used, and Baring kept a special stock of inferior port for the contests, which he labeled "Throwing Port." Two glasses were the only equipment required, for only the port was thrown, not the containers.

The Victorian age was certainly the Golden Age of the parlor game. It is true that many of these games, from Blind Man's Buff and Nine Men's Morris to chess and backgammon, had been played for hundreds of years—the more primitive in village inns and on village greens, the more advanced in the drawing rooms of the wealthy. But it took a large urban middle class, deprived of the village inn, the village hall, and other rural social centers, to develop and popularize the parlor game. To do this it drew on all available sources. Games like charades and Tableaux Vivants, for years popular in the great houses of the rich, were all adapted to the suburban parlor. The ancient game of Nine Men's Morris, or Merels, once played with stones on a playing area marked on the ground, became a board game, as did Fox and Geese and many other old country pastimes.

Children's games were also adapted and developed for parlor gatherings—games whose origins have been lost in antiquity. Most of these, almost certainly, evolved from religious beginnings or primitive customs and survived through the playing activities of children. Children are innately conservative and cling to what they have always known. They also possess a strong sense of the dramatic and prefer games that involve action. It is easy to see, therefore, how games were handed down from generation to generation and changed very little in the process. The game of London Bridge is a good example of such survivals. First the bridge falls down; then it is built up with sticks and stones, then with iron bars, then with silver and gold and so on until the prisoner is taken. This reflects the primitive practice of burying a human sacrifice in the foundations of certain buildings. Again, the game of Oranges and Lemons (although the exact sequence of events is not clear) indicates a contest between opposing parties and an execution.

Then there is the old English country game of Drop Handkerchief, which lost its original meaning before it found its way into the Victorian parlor. Originally a kissing game played at spring fairs, it probably started out as a fertility custom.

Unfortunately for the parlor game, the twentieth century has replaced most recreational activities, both for young and old, with one, single, international preoccupation—television. Instead of playing games ourselves, we watch paid performers play for us: professional sport, professional chess, professional billiards, professional quizzes, professional guessing games. Even Christmas parties are beamed into homes as a substitute for the real thing.

Perhaps a happier and more enlightened generation of the future, having rediscovered that it is satisfying for man to do things for himself, may turn back again to participation. Certainly the craze for electronic games is an indication that this may be so.

Apart from an occasional treatise on "serious" games, such as whist, no book dealing with parlor games appeared until 1825. Thereafter, and up to the end of the century, hundreds of such volumes were published. A book that listed

and described all the games recorded during the period would
be one of encyclopedic proportion. Ruthless pruning has
therefore been the main task in compiling this book.

Several games have been omitted because they are so
trivial and tedious that it is doubtful whether they ever got
beyond the covers of the books in which they appeared. One
example of such a game will suffice:

> Each player is supplied with a saucer and a packet of new
> pins. At a signal, each player must take out all the pins,
> one by one, and then put them back in the holes of the paper
> package. The first to do so is the winner.

I cannot believe that a party of people foregathered to enjoy
themselves would have wasted much time on such humdrum
diversions, especially when they had at their disposal games
as delightful as Wolf and Lamb, Guessing Blind Man, Queen
of Sheba, The Mousetrap, and Poor Pussy, as well as the
various kissing games.

I have omitted games such as tiddlywinks and Halma
because the rules of play are always supplied with the
equipment that is necessary for them; I have also omitted
those games requiring special apparatus that is no longer
available. Games such as bridge and chess are excluded
because so much has been written on them by experts.

A number of pastimes are included that are not strictly
covered by my earlier definition of what constitutes a game,
but which are essentially party games nevertheless. I have
called these Romps. The whole point of a Romp relies upon
the supposed ignorance of the victim, but one's excitement
and pleasure are increased by the very knowledge that, as
victim, one was about to be soaked with water or bumped on
the floor, or suffer some other "misfortune."

In general, my aim has been to present a selection of
old parlor games that includes something for all ages, all
occasions, and all tastes, and I would like to thank all those,
children as well as adults, who have helped me to make this
selection. For many of the card games I am indebted to *The
Cyclopaedia of Card and Table Games* (1891) by Louis
Hoffman, the anonymous *Round Games for all Parties* (1854)
and *Endless Mirth* (1864) by Charles Gilbert.

1

General Party Games

his chapter is devoted to those games whose sole function is to produce merriment. None of them requires the slightest exercise of the intellect. Some are suitable for children, some offer fun to grown-ups, while others may be enjoyed by mixed groups of all ages. Many of them are variations on a theme, and in such cases (Blind Man games, for example) the original themes, well known though they may be, are also given.

Some of the games have no point but are merely exercises in making people laugh. I have often witnessed the most dignified (and sober) persons breaking down helplessly while playing simple games like Poor Pussy. The reader who doubts this is recommended to persuade one of his sterner friends or relations to indulge in a round of Throwing the

Smile or to play The Laughing Game with a straight face.

To those who criticize the prim-and-properness of the Victorians, it may come as a surprise that many of the old parlor games were merely excuses for the exchange of one, or many, amatory salutes. Perhaps such critics have been deceived by the tongue-in-cheek writing style of many Victorians themselves. The anonymous author of *Round Games for All Parties* remarked:

> Great objections exist to the introduction of "kissing" in games. To silence them all—and to keep up that tremendously exalted tone for which our work intends to be celebrated—we hereby announce, that all games requiring the introduction of the objectionable ceremony, are intended by us to be played exclusively in family parties, consisting of brothers, sisters, maiden aunts, grandmothers and uncles. Cousins may be admitted under certain restrictions—but the privilege can extend no further. We hope none of our readers will think of breaking through this regulation.

In compiling this collection, I have studied scores of twentieth-century books on parlor games. Not one of the games described in all these books allows for a single kiss.

BLIND MAN GAMES

Blind Man's Buff: One of the party volunteers to be the first blind man, or is chosen by lot. A handkerchief or scarf is tied over his eyes and he is turned around three times. He then tries to catch any other player he can.

The other players tease him by pushing him, pulling at his clothes, tickling his face with a feather, etc. (The word "buff" is Middle English for a blow or buffet). When he succeeds in seizing someone, the blind man has to guess who it is. If he is right, his prisoner becomes the blind man.

In another version known as French Blind Man's Buff, the blind man's hands are tied behind his back and he is only permitted to walk backward; he captures his prisoner by touching him.

The Bellman: In this version of Blind Man's Buff, *everybody* is blindfolded except one player. He carries a small bell, which he rings from time to time. There is much colliding and

seizing of one blind man by another. The blind man who catches the bellman changes places with him. This game is derived from a much earlier one once played at country fairs in which a belled pig took the place of the player with the bell.

Guessing Blind Man: The players seat themselves on chairs, forming a circle, with the blind man in the center. He is turned around three times, during which maneuver the rest of the players all change seats. The blind man then walks forward and sits on the lap of the first person he contacts and tries to guess who it is.

Should he fail after three attempts, he pays three forfeits (*see* Chapter 6). If he guesses the second time, he pays one forfeit. Should he guess on his first attempt, the person discovered takes his place; otherwise a new blind man is chosen.

According to a handbook of parlor games published in 1844, the blind man (when it *was* a man) always endeavored, through a little preliminary probing, to choose a lady's lap on which to sit, but "a good deal of fun is caused by a young lady throwing her skirt over the lap of the gentleman next to her." This would be difficult today. There is another variety to this game in which the blind man says to the lap's owner, "Can you guess?" which the person asked must repeat. Otherwise the rules remain the same.

Buff with the Wand: In this variant of the time-honored game, the blinded person, stick in hand, stands in the center of the room. The rest of the party join hands in a ring around him and they dance to music. When the music stops, the blind man brings his stick down upon one of the circle, who is then required to grasp its end. The blind one then makes any sound he likes—a street cry, the sound of an animal, or anything else—which the captured person must imitate. Should the blind man guess who holds the stick, he passes the blindfold to the person caught. If not, he must keep the bandage and try again.

Blind Postman: First, a postmaster-general and a postman are appointed. The room furniture is pushed to one side to make space for movement, and the players arrange themselves around the sides of the room. The postmaster-general then tours the room and writes down the players' names, together with the name of a town for each person. The blindfolded postman is then placed in the middle of the room, and the postmaster announces that a letter has been sent from one town to another—say from London to Glasgow. The representatives of these two cities then stand up and as quietly as possible change seats. As they do this, the postman attempts to secure one of the seats himself. If he succeeds, the former occupant of that seat takes on the job of blind postman.

Cat and Mouse: The players sit in two rows facing each other with enough space between the rows to allow one person to pass through. Two are selected as cat and mouse, both of whom are blindfolded. They are placed one at each end of the pathway and may walk around each of the two rows of spectators but must keep within touching distance of them. The object is for the cat to catch the mouse—the hunt being conducted entirely by ear. When the mouse has been caught, another cat and mouse are chosen.

Alice, Where Art Thou?   Each gentleman is given a lady for a partner—*not*, be it noted, the lady of his choice. The gentlemen are then sent out of the room and blindfolded while, in the meantime, the ladies move away from their former positions. The men then return and try to locate their partners. The men may talk but the ladies may not. The winner is the one who first finds his partner.

A variation on this game is to give each lady an animal's name and to permit her to use the call of that creature twice to aid her partner in his search.

Animals: All the players except the blind man station themselves in different parts of the room. The blind man then feels his way around until he touches somebody. That player must at once give an imitation of the noise made by some animal—donkey, cat, dog, cow, pig, cock, repeating it up to three times if requested. The blind man must then guess the name of his prisoner, and if he does so the person named becomes blind man.

Blind Man's Steps: This game, although childishly simple, can be very funny. The blindfolded player is placed in the middle of the room and asked whom he would like to capture (or to kiss). He is then turned to face the object of his choice and told how many steps he must take to make contact. He then inevitably makes absurd mistakes in the direction and the length of the steps he must take.

Isaac and Rebecca: The players, holding hands, form a ring, in which stand Isaac and Rebecca, both blindfolded. Every time he calls out, "Rebecca, where art thou?" she has to reply, "Isaac, here I am" and he endeavors to catch her by following her voice.

Squeak Piggy Squeak: All the players but one sit on chairs in a circle facing inward. The odd player is placed in the middle of the ring, blindfolded, and given a cushion. Holding the cushion in front of him with both hands, the blindfolded player must find a lap by feeling with the cushion, and then, placing it on the lap, sit on it, saying, "Squeak, piggy, squeak." He may demand three squeaks before attempting to identify the piggy. If he is wrong, he must try another lap and go through the same procedure. If and when he succeeds in identifying the piggy, the identified player takes the blindfold and cushion, and the game is resumed.

GAMES WITH CHAIRS

Musical Chairs: A number of chairs (one fewer than the number of players) is placed in a row, facing alternately in

opposite directions. The players march around the chairs in time to music, and when the music stops, every player endeavors to find a seat. The unlucky player without a chair drops out of the game, one more chair is removed, and the game is restarted. Players are not allowed to touch any chair during the march-around. The player who captures the very last remaining chair is the winner.

Musical Potatoes: This is Musical Chairs played without chairs. The players sit in a circle on the floor, all but one holding a potato in his right hand and behind his back. Music is started, and each player passes his potato to the player on his left. When the music stops, the player *without* a potato in his hand is eliminated. One potato is also withdrawn from the game, which then continues on the same principles as Musical Chairs.

Caterpillar: As many chairs as there are players are placed in a circle in the middle of the room, all facing inward. All the players except one seat themselves, while the odd player stands in the middle of the circle. When all the others are settled, the odd man tries to sit down on the vacant chair. The other players try to prevent this by moving onto it—first in one direction, then in the other, so that at one moment the vacant seat may be almost within the odd player's touch and at the next at the very opposite side of the circle. If the seated players move from chair to chair quickly enough, it will be some time before the odd man can sit down. When he does, it is the player on his *left* who takes his place. A most energetic and hilarious game.

Numbers: A number of chairs equal to the number of players is placed in a row. The players seat themselves and are numbered off from left to right. The seats retain these numbers throughout the game. The player seated at the head of the row, that is, number one—calls out another number, say "five." Five must immediately respond by calling out another number and so on.

When a person does not immediately respond to his number, he must go to the foot of the row; all the other players with numbers higher than his (closer to the foot of the row) move up one to make room for him and in so doing change their numbers. Thus seven becomes six and so forth down the line. The length of game is governed either by a time limit or by limiting the number of calls. The player at the head of the row when the game ends is the winner.

Change Seats, the King's Come: As many chairs are placed around the room as will accommodate all the players but one. The seatless one is chosen by lot. When all the rest are seated, the one without a seat stands in the middle and says, "Change seats, change seats, change seats, change seats" as many times as he likes, while all the others remain on the alert for him to add "the King's come."

At this, all the seated players must change seats—but *not* with a neighbor—and the caller tries to obtain a seat for himself. The principal player may sometimes say instead "the King's *not* come," and if he uses this device with some skill, he can cause great confusion as some of the players attempt to change seats while others remain seated. This confusion makes it much easier for him to capture a chair, leaving another player standing to call "change seats."

This is a good version of musical chairs when no music is available. Sir Walter Scott mentions this ancient game in *Rob Roy:* "Here auld ordering and counterordering—but patience! patience!—We may ae day play at *Change seats, the king's coming."*

Sea and Fishes: The players seat themselves in a circle of chairs, leaving one player out, who represents the "sea." The other players having each taken the name of a fish, the sea walks around the circle calling out the names of the fishes one by one. Each player, on hearing his adopted name called out, rises and follows the sea.

When *all* have thus been called (and the sea may have some difficulty in remembering the fish names of all the players), the sea begins to run about crying, "The sea is troubled! The sea is troubled!" The other players still follow until the sea suddenly sits down, an example that must immediately be followed by all the other players. The one who fails to secure a seat becomes the new sea, and the game continues.

How Do You Like Your Neighbors?   The company must seat themselves around the room, leaving plenty of space in the middle in which to move around. One person is left standing in the center and starts the game by asking any other player, "How do you like your neighbors?" The answer must be either "Not at all" or "Very much."

If the reply is "Not at all," the player is asked what other two members of the company he or she would prefer as neighbors, and these must immediately change places with the unwanted ones. During the change, the questioner must try to secure one of the vacated seats and leave one of the four as the next questioner. If the answer is "Very much," then *all* the players must change seats, leaving one of them as the interrogator.

HUNTING GAMES

Hunt the Slipper: All the players but one sit on the floor in a circle with their legs crossed, one acting as the chief cobbler, and all the other seated players pretending to mend shoes. The odd player brings a slipper to the chief cobbler and asks for it to be mended, saying:

> *"Cobbler, cobbler, mend my shoe,*
> *Get it done by half past two."*

After turning his back for a moment, the slipper hunter demands its return, but is told that it has been lost. He then starts to search for it. The cobblers all place their hands behind their backs and pass the slipper secretly from one to the other. The slipper hunter can demand to see the hands of any one cobbler at any time until he finds it. The last holder of the slipper then becomes its owner.

Hunt the Thimble: Everyone leaves the room except the thimble hider, who places the thimble in a place where it can be seen without moving other objects. The players then enter the room all together and walk around hunting the thimble. No word is spoken, but when anyone sees the thimble, he sits down without indicating where it is. The last player to sit down pays a forfeit.

Hunt the Ring: A ring or a small key is threaded onto a long piece of string, which is then fastened to form a circle. The company then stand in a circle all holding the string and pass the ring from hand to hand while the hunter, standing in the middle, tries to guess in whose hand the ring is. It is, of course, only passed when the hunter's back is turned. Whoever is caught with the ring takes his place in the middle of the circle.

Hot Boiled Beans: One player is sent out of the room, and a small article is hidden. When this has been done, the absent player is told, "Hot boiled beans and bacon for supper, hurry up before it gets cold." On hearing this the player returns to the room and searches for the missing article while the rest of the company inform him that his supper is getting "very cold," "cold," "warmer," "hot," "very hot," or is "burning," according to how far or near he is from the article to be found.

GUESSING GAMES

Who Am I? Each player in turn secretly assumes the identity of a famous person, living or dead. It is the task of the others to discover this identity by asking questions. The celebrity must only answer yes or no.

Q. Are you a man?
A. No.
Q. Are you living?
A. No.
Q. Are you an actress?

And so on until the identity is discovered as being Florence Nightingale, Lucrezia Borgia, Helen of Troy, Molly Pitcher, or whom have you.

In a variant of this game, one player leaves the room while the others invest him with an identity. He then returns, and the game proceeds in reverse, as it were, the celebrity asking the company, "Am I a man?" etc.

Yes or No: In this game one person leaves the room while his friends fix upon an object word for him to discover. When he is recalled, he may ask any number of questions to try to discover the word, but the answers given him must be simply yes or no—nothing more.

Another version of this game simply reverses the procedure. One of the company, without leaving the room, thinks of an object to be guessed at by the remainder of those present. Again, he may only answer yes or no.

The Object Game: This is a variation of the game now famous as *Twenty Questions* and is more suitable than the latter when a party of twelve or more are playing. The party is divided into two equal teams. One person from each team is sent outside, and between them they decide on the object that the others must guess.

The players then arrange themselves in two distinct circles far enough away from one another so that the remarks of one side cannot be overheard by the other. The two representatives then take their places within the respective circles, and a race begins to discover the secret word. The rules of the game stipulate that the number of questions each side may ask should be limited to twenty, though usually it is impossible to enforce this without two other players acting as referees.

One rule must be strictly adhered to, however, and that is that the answers given to the questioners are limited to yes or no. If a question is asked that cannot be answered with a simple positive or negative, then it must not be answered at all. The team that arrives at the correct word first is, of course, the winning one.

How, Why, When and Where: One player thinks of the name of an object—any object—it being the task of the other players to discover what it is by asking (only once) the following four questions:

"How do you like it?"
"Why do you like it?"
"When do you like it?"
"Where do you like it?"

The first player is entitled to think of a word that has more than one meaning and to confuse his questioners by using a different meaning to make each reply. Thus—male (masculine), mail (letters), and mail (armor):

"How do you like it?" "When it's a good friend."
"Why do you like it?" "Because it sometimes
brings good news."
"When do you like it?" "First thing in the morning."
"Where do you like it?" "In a museum."

Throwing up Lights: In this game two players secretly decide upon a word and then carry on a conversation between themselves which will throw some light upon what the word is. The object of the game is for the other players to guess the word by listening to the conversation.

If a player thinks that he has discovered the word, he calls out, "I strike a light," and then whispers his guess into the ear of one of the leaders. If he has guessed correctly, he joins in the conversation, and the remaining players continue to try to detect the word. If, on the other hand, he has mistaken the word, he must sit on the floor with a handkerchief over his face until the end of the game or until he guesses the word correctly.

Smells: This game needs to be prepared beforehand. You need a number of small vessels—cups, glasses, or jam jars—each containing one substance that gives off an odor. Shoe polish, some vinegar, some kerosine, a piece of apple, some custard powder—the list of available substances is almost endless. Needless to say, substances such as orange, gasoline, ammonia, etc., which have highly characteristic odors should not be used.

The players are sent out of the room, and one by one they reenter to be blindfolded. Each dish is then presented to the player's nose, and he must guess what it contains. When his attempts are finished, he stays to watch the fun as the other members of the party try their luck—and luck it usually is, as will be demonstrated to any who play this game. Strawberry jam, for instance, can, when not seen, be quite easily mistaken for cleaning fluid, lemonade, or even hair spray.

A modern version of this game is to prerecord onto tape a number of common sounds and to use these instead of "smells." I think the original game is far better.

Recognition: For this game a prepared list of objects is required. It can either be duplicated beforehand, according to the number of expected players, or the list may be dictated to the players, each of whom will write it down. The players must, within a time limit, record what famous person— mythical, fictional, or historical—each object suggests. A possible list might be as follows:

A cherry tree	George Washington
A muddy cloak	Sir Walter Raleigh
A bucket of whitewash	Tom Sawyer
A burning bush	Moses
A footprint in the sand	Robinson Crusoe
A glass slipper	Cinderella
A parrot	Long John Silver
A stovepipe hat	Abraham Lincoln
A magic sword or a round table	King Arthur

The list can, of course, be varied to suit the average age of the party.

Stool of Repentance: One member of the party is sent out of the room while the rest each make a criticism of him or her. These are noted down by one of the players. A stool or chair is set up in the middle of the room, and the penitent is called in and stood upon it.

The criticisms are then read out to him one by one, thus: "Somebody says you are conceited—who?" and the victim has to guess the name of his critic. Then he is told that someone considers him greedy or ugly and so on. If he guesses a sufficient (prearranged) number of his critics, he is absolved and joins the circle for the next round; otherwise he pays a forfeit. In theory, he should undergo the ordeal again, but as the game ceases to be amusing if the same person is twice dealt with, he is usually considered to have earned his release whether he guesses correctly or not.

Shadow Buff: A large white sheet is pinned against a wall of the room while on a table some distance away from it, a bright light is placed. One player sits on the floor facing the sheet, with his back to the light. All other lights in the room are extinguished, and the remainder of the company pass one by one behind the watcher, who has to identify each by his shadow. Gestures may be used, masks or false noses worn, in fact any device may be employed to confuse the guesser. Those whose identity is successfully discovered must pay a forfeit.

CHASING AND CATCHING GAMES

Hare and Hound: The players stand in a circle in twos, one behind the other. Two are left out, the hare and the hound, and the game is for the hound to catch the hare, who runs around the circle until, when he chooses, he can stand in front of one of the pairs, thereby making it a three.

As soon as he does this, the back one of the three becomes the hare and must run away from the hound. The hound must continue chasing each successive hare until he catches one, but he must not touch him if he is standing in front of another. If caught, the hare, of course, must become the hound.

Frog in the Middle: One player sits on the floor with his legs under him; the others form a ring around. Then they prod, push, or pull the frog, who tries to catch one of them without rising from the floor or changing his position in the center of the ring. The one who is caught becomes the frog.

I Wrote a Letter to My Love, or Kiss in the Ring: All except one of the party form a ring and hold hands. The player left outside the ring (the postman) walks around, touching each of the players with a handkerchief while chanting the following lines:

> *"I wrote a letter to my love,*
> *But on the way I dropped it.*
> *One of you has picked it up,*
> *And put it in your pocket."*

Having selected one of the circle, the postman drops the handkerchief behind him and runs around the ring. The player behind whom the handkerchief has been dropped leaves his place and tries to catch the postman before he can occupy the vacant space in the circle.

The two players can dart under the uplifted arms of the other players, and sometimes the circle may obstruct either the hunter or the hunted. If the postman is not caught before he occupies the vacant space, the chaser becomes the postman, and the game starts again. If caught, the postman gives a forfeit.

Hand in, Hand out: This game is similar to the preceding one. It is played by young people who form a circle. One of them, chosen by lot, walks around the group and, if a boy, strikes a girl, or, if a girl, strikes a boy. Then, the striker and the struck run in pursuit of each other until the latter is caught and becomes the striker for the next round.

Moving Statues, or Grandmother's Footsteps: This game can be played indoors, although it is better done outdoors. One player stands at the end of the room (or lawn), and the other players have to advance on him while his back is turned. He may turn around suddenly at whatever intervals he likes, and when he does so, the other players must immediately become petrified. Any of them detected making the slightest movement must go back to the starting line and begin again. The first person who gets near enough to touch "it" is the winner, and, if the game is to be continued, becomes "it" himself.

"BE SERIOUS" GAMES

Throwing the Smile: The players sit around in a circle, and *one* of them smiles for a moment or so. He then wipes his hand across his face to wipe off the smile and pretends to throw it to another player of his choice, who has to catch it with his hand, put it on, wear it for a while, and wipe it off to throw to someone else. Anyone who smiles out of turn is out, and the last player remaining wins the game. Those players who are "out" will laugh heartily as the game proceeds, thus making it more and more difficult for the remaining players to stay "in."

Poor Pussy: All the players sit in a circle except pussy. When all are seated, pussy walks around on hands and knees and adopts a begging posture at the feet of one of the circle. Pussy looks as pathetic as possible and gives a pitiful "meow." The one appealed to must say "poor pussy" in as consoling a way as possible, but without the shadow of a smile. This is repeated three times, and if a smile appears on either face, a forfeit is paid, and pussy and the other player change places.

The Laughing Game: The players seat themselves in a circle and the first player begins the game by saying, "ha." The next player must say, "ha, ha," and the third, "ha, ha, ha." All must be pronounced with the utmost solemnity, and any player exhibiting the faintest sign of hilarity is expelled from the circle with a forfeit to his name. This game doesn't usually last long, for the entire circle is usually doubled up before "Ha, ha, ha" is reached.

Buff Says Baff: This is the oldest of all the "no laughing" games, for it is mentioned as being ancient in a book of parlor games published in the 1850's. One of the company leaves the room on a supposed visit to Buff. He returns carrying a broomstick (or umbrella) and is asked by the company:

Q.   Where do you come from?
A.   From Buff!
Q.   Did he say anything to you?
A.   Buff said, "Baff!"
     And he gave me this staff,
     Telling me neither to smile nor laugh.
     Buff says, "Baff," to all his men,
     And I say, "Baff," to you again,
     And he neither laughs nor smiles,
     In spite of all your cunning wiles,
     But carries his face with a very good grace
     And passes his stick to the very next place.

The stick is then passed to another player, and so on.
Any player coming from Buff who so much as smiles during
this performance has to pay a forfeit.

Pinch Without Laughing: In this extremely simple game
each player pinches the nose of his neighbor, who must
submit to the operation without laughing. If he so much as
smiles, he pays a forfeit. The nose pinchers are permitted to
use all their comic ingenuity in the attempt to induce the
pinchee to lose his gravity.

Statues: The players dance around the room in couples
with some degree of abandon until the music suddenly stops.
Then the dancers must immediately freeze, holding the pose
no matter what their attitude may be. Any player who moves
or even smiles is disqualified. Then the music and the game

resume—until in the end only one couple remains.

The Sculptor: One player acting as the sculptor arranges all the other players into various postures—the more absurd, the better. These postures must be retained without movement. The sculptor then goes around to each person, endeavoring to make him laugh or smile. Of course the players must remain absolutely immobile. The sculptor may resort to any device to create mirth or movement short of touching anyone. The first player to move or laugh gives up a forfeit and himself becomes the sculptor.

TALKING GAMES

Black Cap and Red Cap: This old game relies for its fun on the quickness of the questioner and the other players, as questions and answers must follow each other with great rapidity.

The questioner gives the name of a cap of a particular color to all the other players: black Cap, red Cap, blue Cap, yellow Cap, and so on. The players then sit in a row on the floor, with the questioner in front of them. Each cap, on hearing his name mentioned, either by the questioner or by one of the other players, must instantly start to his feet and answer under pain of forfeit. All players must use the appropriate language; the omission of the prefix "sir" or "madam" incurs a severe forfeit, as does the slightest variation in the form of the answers. The game proceeds thus:

> *Questioner* (looking severe): What's this? Somebody's been at the strawberries! Can you tell me who it was, Red Cap?
> *Red Cap* (on his feet):   Yes, sir; it was Blue Cap.
> *Blue Cap* (starting up):   Who, sir? I, sir?
> *Questioner:*   Yes, sir; don't you hear, sir?
> *Blue Cap:*   Oh, no, sir; not me, sir; it was Yellow Cap.
> *Yellow Cap:*   Who, sir? I, sir?

The game continues until all the players but one have been eliminated by making a mistake.

The Prince of Paris: This is a variation of thé preceding game. All the players but one are given a number from 1

upward and the numberless player takes the lead. Standing
in front, he says, "The Prince of Paris has lost his hat. Did
you find it, Number Six, sir?" Number Six must now stand
up and answer, "What, sir! I, sir?"

Leader: Yes, sir! You, sir!
No. Six: Not I, sir!
Leader: Who then, sir?
No. Six: Number One, sir!
No. One (getting up): What, sir! I, sir?
Leader: Yes, sir! You, sir!
No. One: Not I, sir!
Leader: Who then, sir?
No. One: Number Eight, sir! (and so on)

The rules and penalties of the game are identical to those of
Black Cap and Red Cap.

Priest Cap: Yet another version of Black Cap. All the
players sit in a line, and each is given a number—one, two,
three, etc.—each keeping that number throughout the
game. The priest then says, "I call upon Number Seven," or
whatever number he likes, and Number Seven must answer
"Not I, sir" before the priest can count five. If he fails to do
so, he must go to the bottom of the line, but if he answers in
time, the priest asks him, "Who then?" to which Number
Seven must reply some other number, and the number thus
called goes through the same process.
     The idea of the game is for the ladies to get all the men
at the bottom of the row, while the men do their best to send
the ladies there. The difficulty, of course, is in remembering
the numbers of all the others. For instance, if Number
Seven, in answer to the question, "Who then?" gives the
number of the one already at the end of the row, he must take
the bottom place himself. If the game is played quickly, it is
very exciting.

Family Coach: This must be a very old game indeed, for its
antiquity is remarked upon in many early Victorian com-
pendiums of games. It appears and reappears over the
decades and has recently been included in a book of indoor
games under the name of Family Car. The coach version is
given here.
     Each person takes the name of a character in a story that
is improvised; they also take the name of a part of the family

coach. One person stands up and tells the story, and as the names or parts are mentioned, the different people holding these names must stand up, turn around, and sit down again. Whenever the family coach is mentioned, the entire company must rise and change seats, while the teller of the story tries to secure a seat for himself, leaving the odd man out to continue the story.

Mr. Wiggins	The Box
Mrs. Wiggins	Rumble-tumble
Aunt Ellen	Axle tree
Miss Jemima	Springs
Captain Tobacco	Door
Master Harry	Wheels
Coachman	Windows
Juba	Perch
Chloe	Steps
The horses	Reins
The little dog	Whip

The Tale

A family party had agreed to take a pleasure jaunt from London to Richmond. The party consisted of Mr. and Mrs. Wiggins, Aunt Ellen, Master Harry, Miss Jemima, and Captain Tobacco. It was proposed by Mr. Wiggins, in order that they might see the country better, that they should all travel together in the family coach.

Mr. Wiggins soon arranged that he and Mrs. Wiggins, Aunt Ellen, her dear little dog, Miss Jemima, and Captain Tobacco should take their seats inside, while Master Harry should ride on the box with the coachman, and Juba and Chloe, the two servants, should take their places in the rumble-tumble. Since everyone was perfectly satisfied with Mr. Wiggins' arrangement, the luggage was speedily packed under the box and beneath the rumble-tumble, while a few more articles belonging to Aunt Ellen and Miss Jemima were carefully stowed away in the seat of the family coach.

Everything was ready. Juba flung open the door, the steps were let down, the windows shut, the ladies took their seats, the coachman took the reins and mounted the box, with Harry by his side. "All right!" cried Captain Tobacco, and off they would have gone in half a twinkling had not Aunt Ellen called out, "But where's the little dog?"

A search was made, and Juba soon found him rolled up under the rumble-tumble. Chloe pulled him out, and he was forthwith placed under the special care of Aunt Ellen inside the family coach. And so forth.

The story given above is only an example. The storyteller makes his own up as he goes along, until he manages to unseat another player, who then picks up the thread of the narrative and carries it on.

The Artist: One player takes the part of the Artist, the rest of the company are colors, each taking a name—blue, green, orange, etc. When a player hears his own color mentioned, he must respond by naming another color. In addition there are four words that are answered by all the company. If the artist mentions the word "colors," all say, "Here we are." If he says "pencil," they say, "Brush! brush!" If he speaks of his "palette," they answer with "Colors! colors!" and if he names "turpentine," the colors show signs of alarm and cry out, "Help! help!" Finally any color named by another color must reply, "Here, sir." Mistakes or hesitations are punished by forfeits. The example we give is one hundred years old.

Artist: I am commissioned by my noble patron, the Marquis of Carabas, to paint a picture of the *finding of the body of Harold.* It is a very important matter. I have made my design, and shall now commence setting my palette.
All the colors: Colors! Colors!.
Artist: I intend to astonish the critics by the brilliancy of my colors.
All: Here we are!
Artist: I can't employ you all at a time—rather a task for a single pencil.
All: Brush! brush!
Artist: Silence! or I'll exterminate you with a dose of turpentine.
All: Help! help!
Artist: I'll begin with the eyes of the fair Edith. They ought to be black. (If the artist names a color not in the collection, he pays a forfeit. The same rule applies to the players who are colors.)
Black: Green! Green!
Green: Here, sir.
Artist: No. She was called Edith the Fair. They must have been blue.
Blue: Orange! Orange!
Orange: Here, sir.

Artist: As she was in trouble, her cheeks ought to be pale—almost white.
White: Purple and Cherry.
Purple and Cherry (together): Here, sir.
Artist: All the colors—
All: Here we are!
Artist: —of the rainbow, and thanks to the delicacy of my pencil—
All: Brush! Brush! (etc., etc.)

The game should be played at a good pace. Forfeits are exacted for mistakes or the slightest hesitations.

What's the Price of Barley? The conductor of the game is called the master, and he gives to the players any names he likes, consisting of simple words, such as these:

Player No. 1: Jack
Player No. 2: How much?
Player No. 3: What?
Player No. 4: Too much!
Player No. 5: Hooray
Player No. 6: Fifty cents
Player No. 7: Two bits
Player No. 8: Eighteen cents
Player No. 9: Good
Player No. 10: Nonsense

The game is carried on in dialogue, starting with the master, in the following manner:

Master: Jack!
No. 1: Yes, master.
Master: What's the price of barley?
No. 1: Fifty cents.
(No. 6 must *not* respond here, his name not having been called by the master. If he does, and he probably will, he pays a forfeit.)
Master: Good!
No. 9: Yes, master.
Master: What's the price of barley?
No. 9: Eighteen cents.
Master: Eighteen cents! Nonsense!
8 & 10: Yes, master.
Master: How much?
No. 2: Yes, master.
Master: What's the price of barley?

No. 2:   Two bits.

Master: Two bits! Hooray! Jack!

7, 5 & 1:   (together):   Yes, master.

Master: What's the price of barley?

7, 5 & 1:   Two bits, fifty cents, eighteen cents (or as they feel inclined).

Master: Nonsense!

No. 10:   Yes, master. (Etc., etc.)

Played briskly, this game never fails to produce a splendid collection of forfeits.

My Lady's Toilet: All the players adopt the name of the various articles connected with the mystery of a Victorian lady's toilet, such as buckles, bouquet, fan, gloves, necklace, bracelet, brooch, etc. "It" is called the spinner; he holds a plate or Frisbee or other flat, spinnable object. The spinner says, "My lady is going to dress for a ball and wants —————— [her *gloves*, her *earrings*, or any other article agreed upon]. As he pronounces the word, the spinner gives the object a twist and the player called upon darts from his seat (which is taken by the spinner) and tries to catch the object before it falls to the ground.

Forfeits reward failures. The spinner may occasionally vary the proceedings by, instead of naming a particular article, making use of the word *toilet*. At this signal all players change places, the speaker rushing for the nearest chair. Anyone found after the scuffle in the same place as before pays a forfeit, as must also the player who is left without a seat at all; the latter takes the next spin.

The spinner may also use the word "*twilight*," as, for instance, by saying; "My lady is going out this evening at . . . *twilight.*" At this, no one is allowed to move on pain of forfeit. The similarity of the two words "twilight" and "toilet" usually leads to a general melee.

This Is My Eye: One player starts the game by touching his eye and saying that it is something else. The next player (who must be called by name) touches the part named and calls it something else.

1st Player (touching his eye):   This is my thumb, George.

George (touching thumb):   This is my chin, Jill.

Jill (touching chin):   This is my nose, Anthony.

Anthony (touching nose):   This is my ear, Sally.

Sally (touching ear): This is my ear, Mark.

MISTAKE: Sally is out.

Many mistakes are made if the game is played rapidly. Two mistakes are allowed each player, and the last one in is the winner.

Russian Gossip: This is a game from which more than one lesson can be learned—the more so if there are a good many players. First of all a circle is formed. Then one player whispers into the ear of his neighbor some little incident, real or imaginary, an anecdote or a piece of gossip. The receiver of the news then whispers it to the next player and so on, around the circle, until it returns to its source. It is then repeated aloud and compared with its original, to which it will often bear no resemblance whatsoever.

Buzz: This game requires all a player's wits; otherwise he will find himself out very early in the proceedings. The first player says "one," the next "two," the next "three," and so on until seven is reached. Instead of saying "seven," the player whose turn it is must say "buzz." At every multiple of seven—14, 21, 28, 35, 42, etc.—the word "buzz" must be substituted as it must in every number containing a seven—17, 27, 37, etc. At 77, the player should say, "buzz-buzz." Any player who fails to "buzz" is out of the game, the last player being the winner.

Prophecies: All that is required for this little frolic is a certain amount of tact on the part of the players. The game is only effective when the members of the company are fairly well acquainted. Early on in the proceedings, all write down on pieces of paper, privately, a prediction concerning some other member of the party—that is, something he or she will do or say during the course of the evening. Before the party breaks up, the prophecies are read aloud to be refuted or confirmed—usually the latter.

ACTION AND MOVEMENT GAMES

The Trades: A very old game and a very good one. Each player except one selects a trade which he carries on in pantomime as follows:

The tailor stitches a coat.
The cobbler mends a shoe.
The laundress washes a tub of linen.
The painter paints a portrait.
The blacksmith hammers at his anvil, etc.

The remaining player is the jack of all trades and he starts the game by exercising whatever trade he pleases (except one already chosen by another player). In doing this, he sets an example of industry to all the others, who must then work away at their own various callings.

Now, the jack of all trades is also a master of all trades, so he can, whenever it pleases him, change his trade and adopt that of another of the party. When this happens, all leave off work at once, except the player thus imitated, who immediately takes up the trade the jack has just left off and continues to exercise it until such time as the jack decides to change again and to take up the work of yet another player. This worker then takes up the jack's trade and continues until another change is made, the other players remaining idle until the jack resumes his original occupation, which is a signal for all to get back to work. Mistakes earn forfeits.

Flying: The players seat themselves each with his right hand placed on his left arm. The game leader sits in front and tells a story that includes as many animals as possible (he may, if he prefers, merely recite a list of animals). The point of the game is that every time a flying creature is mentioned, each right hand must be raised and fluttered in the air in imitation of flying.

This once very popular party game is not quite as simple as might first appear. Many birds—the ostrich, penguin, and emu, for instance—cannot fly, whereas bats, which are not birds, do fly. Some insects fly, others do not, and if the game is played fairly rapidly, many forfeits will be taken.

Fishermen: This centuries-old game was introduced to the English parlor from Russia at about the turn of the last century. Each player fastens to his back a piece of heavy thread but light enough to snap off if stepped upon. It should be just long enough to trail on the floor, and on the loose end will be fastened some small object, such as an empty spool of thread or a pencil or anything heavy enough to trail.

On the signal to begin, each player tries to step on the other players' "fish," so as to snap the thread and allow the first player to pick it up. At the same time, he tries to save his own fish from being caught. No player must touch any fish line (and this includes his own) with his hands. As each player loses his fish, he retires from the game, and the catcher of the most fish is the winner.

Feather: A small, fluffy feather is required to play this game. The players draw their chairs into a close circle. One of the party throws the feather into the air as high as possible. He then blows upon it to keep it floating in the air. The player to whom it comes nearest does the same, in order to prevent it from touching him—an accident that demands from him a forfeit. One of the joys of this game is the spectacle of the players trying to blow while laughing—a quite impossible operation. This very simple game is recommended as a great producer of both helpless laughter and forfeits.

Potato Race: A number of potatoes and as many spoons and baskets (or other receptacles) are required. The baskets are arranged about a yard apart on one side of the room, and from each basket a number of potatoes are placed at intervals of a foot or so to the opposite side.

Each player is given a spoon and his task is to spoon up all the potatoes on his line and put them into his basket. The potatoes must be picked up and carried with the spoon alone and must not be touched by any part of the body. If a potato is dropped en route to its basket, it must be picked up (with the spoon) carried to its starting place and put back on the floor, and the player must begin again. The first player to get all his potatoes into his basket is the winner.

Hot Cockles: One player kneels down, hiding his eyes by laying his head on a chair. He puts one hand behind him, palm uppermost, which the other players strike with their hands. The simple point of this game is for the kneeling player to guess who strikes him. When he is successful, the striker takes his place.

This game was noticed by John Gay:

> *As at hot-cockles once I laid me down,*
> *I felt the weighty hand of many a clown;*
> *Buxoma gave a gentle tap, and I*
> *Quick rose and read soft mischief in her eye.*

Pinning the Tail on the Donkey: This most unsophisticated of all parlor games still causes much merriment. The necessary equipment—the picture of a tailless donkey together with his missing appendage—can still be purchased. Each player stands about six feet from the donkey, is given the tail, and is blindfolded. The purpose of the game is obvious.

Another method of play is to have a number of tails, all marked with a number. As each tail is positioned it is left in place, while the next player takes his turn. When all have made their attempt, the player who pinned his tail nearest to its correct position is the winner.

Blowing Out the Candle: This is a game similar to pinning the tail on the donkey. A candle is placed on a table, and each player in turn is placed a few feet away from it and blindfolded. His task is to advance toward the candle and to blow it out within the space of time that it takes the rest of the company to count to twenty in unison.

The attempts of the blindfolded one cause much laughter, which infects him and makes his attempts to pursue his lips for blowing ludicrous in the extreme. Failure to extinguish the candle means a forfeit, and it is only the player with an iron-disciplined mind and an unerring sense of direction who gets through the game unscathed.

The Cushion Dance: A cushion is placed in the middle of the room, around which the players, (previously arranged into two sides), form a circle with joined hands. They circle the cushion a few times, and then one side tries to pull the other side forward so as to force one of its number to touch the cushion with his foot.

The ensuing struggle is usually fairly intense, and ultimately someone's foot touches the cushion, and that person has to leave the circle. When one side has been completely eliminated, the other side is proclaimed as the winner.

O'Grady Says: This game (similar to Simon Says and May I?) invariably results in a rich crop of forfeits. One of the players takes command under the name of "O'Grady," and everything O'Grady says must be obeyed or a forfeit given.

It must be remembered that every order to be obeyed must be preceded with the words "O'Grady says." The game proceeds as follows: "O'Grady says do this" (raising a hand, for example). The players follow suit. Then "O'Grady says do this" (he does something else). Then "Do this!" This command must be ignored, on pain of forfeit.

The Rule of Contrary: The rules of the game are simple. All the players, standing up, take hold of a large square scarf. One player, taking hold with the rest, starts the game by saying:

> *"Here we go by the rule of contrary;*
> *When I say, 'Hold fast,' let go;*
> *When I say, 'Let go,' hold fast."*

He then says "Let go" or "Hold fast" as he chooses. When he says, "Let go," all those who do so pay a forfeit; when he says, "Hold fast," all who do not let go are similarly punished. It may be thought that few fall victim to such a simple contrivance, but the game usually produces its fair share of the party's forfeits.

Opposites: The guests are arranged in a semicircle, each with a chair behind him. One of them moves from person to person, either performing some action or giving some instruction. The person concerned must do the exact opposite. If told to raise his right leg, he raises his left; if instructed to take off his hat, he must put it on. One by one the players will drop out, and the one who holds out the longest is the winner.

Who's the Leader?   All the players stand in a circle except one, who is sent out of the room. A leader is appointed, whose duty it is to lead the other players in clapping, foot-tapping, knee-bending, or any other movement that may occur to him. The players engage in the first movement, say clapping, and the absent player is recalled. It is his task to discover who is leading the players in their actions.

When the leader thinks the moment is opportune, the leader changes the action from clapping to, say, twiddling his thumbs, and the rest of the players follow suit. The players should keep their eyes off the leader as much as possible. It is surprising how quickly the new movement spreads and how difficult it is to discover the leader.

When he *is* discovered, the leader is sent out, and a new one is selected. This games improves if the actions are done in time to music. There are no forfeits involved, and nobody wins or loses.

Sardines: Like Hide and Seek, Sardines is played in the dark and in as many rooms as possible. One player goes away and hides, and the rest spread out to look for him. The hiding place chosen should have a reasonable amount of room.

The first seeker to find the hider joins him in the same place, both remaining as quiet as possible. The next successful seeker joins them, again as noiselessly as possible, and so on. The game ends when all the sardines but one are wedged into the closet or whatever, and the last to discover the hiding place pays a forfeit.

Spinning the Trencher: This game is found in all the earliest parlor-game books and was evidently very popular. It is simple enough. All the players sit around the room making as large a circle as possible. The player who starts holds a circular wooden bread board or tray, which is the "trencher."

Standing in the middle of the circle, he spins it on its edge, while at the same time calling out the name of another player. The named player must spring up and catch the trencher before it ceases to spin. Failure to do this involves a forfeit. It often happens—particularly when the spinner looks hard at one person and calls the name of another—that the wrong person jumps up and bumps into the other.

Moving Statues: In this game, all but two players leave the room and between them form a statue group, which remains quite motionless. One player is then called in and makes suggestions for "improving" the statue. His suggestions will undoubtedly be absurd.

When he has done this, he is compelled to take the most ludicrous position in the group himself, the player who is now free remaining to see the fun. Another player is then summoned, and the process repeated. The game continues thus with an ever-increasing number of spectators inside and an ever-decreasing number of budding sculptors outside.

Nuts in May: This is suitable for young players and is a very pretty game. Two sides are chosen and a line is drawn across the middle of the room. The children arrange themselves in two rows, one on either side of the line, facing one another.

The game is begun by one row advancing toward the other with joined hands, singing:

> *"Here we come gathering nuts in May, nuts in May,*
> *nuts in May,*
> *Here we come gathering nuts in May, on a cold*
> *and frosty morning."*

They then retreat to their original position, and the opposite side advances, singing in reply:

> *"Pray, who will you gather for nuts in May, nuts*
> *in May, nuts in May?*
> *Pray who will you gather for nuts in May, on a*
> *cold and frosty morning?"*

The first row then settles upon some player on the opposite side, and again advances, singing:

> *"We'll gather Edna [or Mary or whomever] for nuts in May,*
> *nuts in May, nuts in May,"* etc.

The other side then sings:

> *"Pray, who will you send to fetch her away,"* etc.

Then, after deciding whom they will send, the first side sings:

> *"We will send Ernest to fetch her away,*
> *fetch her away, fetch her away,*
> *We will send Ernest to fetch her away,*
> *on a cold and frosty morning."*

The girl must then stand on one side of the line, and the boy on the other, each trying to pull the other over it. If Ernest wins, Edna will have to join his row; if Edna wins, Ernest must join her party. Either way the singing begins again.

Orange and Lemons: This is a slightly different version of the familiar London Bridge. Two of the company, one pretending to be an Englishman and the other a Frenchman, stand face to face holding each other's hands. They form an arch for the rest to pass through, one by one. As the players pass under the bridge, the couple forming it sing the famous rhyme.

> *"Oranges and lemons,*
> *Sang the bells of St. Clements.*
> *You owe me five farthings,*
> *Sang the bells of St. Martin's.*
> *When will you pay me?*
> *Sang the bells of Old Bailey.*
> *When I grow rich,*
> *Sang the bells of Shoreditch.*
> *When will that be?*
> *Sang the bells of Stepney.*
> *That I don't know,*
> *Sang the great bell of Bow.*
> *Gay go up and gay go down,*
> *To ring the bells of London Town."*

Then, accelerating their tempo, the bridge makers chant:

> *"Here comes a candle to light you to bed,*
> *And here comes a chopper to chop off your head."*

At this they bring down their hands to capture a player. The prisoner is asked whether he is English or French and has to whisper his choice to his captors, who then place him on either the French or the English side—these sides being known only to the bridge builders. When all the players have been captured and allocated to one or other of the armies, the latter form two waist-held lines and hold a tug-of-war. The strongest army is the side that pulls its opponents across a given line.

Jack's Alive: This game should be reserved for adults only. A twist of paper is set alight and the flame blown out to leave a burning ember. This paper is then handed from player to player, each saying, as they present it,

> *"Jack's alive, and likely to live;*
> *If he dies in your hand, you've a forfeit to give."*

(If preferred, only the words "Jack's Alive" may be used.) The player in whose hand the spark expires duly pays a forfeit, for which reason, when Jack is looking tolerably healthy, the players are in no hurry to pass him around but take their time in making the pronouncement. As he grows weaker, however, his circulation becomes very rapid indeed, as does the spoken formula.

Snapdragon: This is a very old game and was still popular in the 1930's. A quantity of raisins is placed in a bowl and covered with sufficient brandy to soak them thoroughly. The bowl is placed in the center of the room, the lights are put out, and the brandy is set alight. (The dish should be on a small table covered with newspaper or oilcloth.)

The point of the game is, believe it or not, for the children to snatch the flaming raisins (or snapdragons) from the dish. Flames made by burning brandy have very little heat in them and only a very clumsy player could sustain the slightest burn, while quickness and dexterity will be rewarded with a great many snapdragons. Still, this is a game that obviously requires close adult supervision.

Battledore and Shuttlecock: Battledores, which resemble small tennis rackets, can still be bought, or table-tennis paddles can be used as a substitute. The object of the game is simply to keep the shuttlecock in the air for as long as possible—either solo or between a number of players. A balloon makes a good substitute for the shuttlecock.

Drawing-room Tennis with Japanese Fans and Air Balloons.

ACTING GAMES

Charades: This old form of the most famous of all parlor games was already established as a favorite pastime in the eighteenth century. The origin of the word is doubtful but it is likely that it derives either from the Provencal *charra*, "to chatter," or from the Spanish *charrada*, "the speech or action of a clown."

All that is required to act a charade are a few pieces of clothing, maybe an odd item of furniture or two and various

"props" that can be adapted from ordinary household odds
and ends. All else that is needed is a few bright people, not
unduly introverted, who will act out the plays.

   The actors decide on the word to be acted. It must have
two or more syllables, each of which has a meaning of its
own—"nutmeg" or "waterfall," for example. If the latter
word is chosen, three little plays are improvised: the first
containing the word "water," the second "fall," and the last
containing the complete word "waterfall." The object of the
game is for the members of the audience to guess the word.

   The following are a few of the words suitable for charade
acting: arrowroot, artichoke, bookworm, brimstone,
cowslip, cupboard, cutlet, daybreak, dovetail, earshot,
farewell, footman, grandchild, handsome, hardship, helpless, indulgent, inmate, intent, joyful, kindred, lawful,
lifelike, loophole, milkmaid, mistake, misunderstand,
necklace, nightmare, nutmeg, orphanage, outside, padlock,
painful, pilgrim, quicklime, quicksand, ragamuffin,
ringleader, roundhead, scarlet, season, sofa, starling, state-
ment, sweetmeat, sweetheart, tendon, threshold, toadstool,
triplet, upright, uproar, vampire, vanguard, waistcoat,
waterfall, wedlock, willful, workmanship, youthful and, for
good measure, zealot and zestful (though not, by the way,
words like zoological, which instantly betray themselves).

   For three or more word charades we suggest the following:

artificial	Art-I-Fish-All
persuaded	Purse-Wade-Ed
understandable	Under-Stand-Able
perspicacity	Purse-Pick-A-City
seasonable	Sea-Son-Able
culmination	Cull-My-Nation
intrusive	In-True-Sieve

Tableaux Vivants ("Living Pictures"):   Neither speaking, acting, nor miming talents are required for this old pastime. The party divides into two or more groups of three or four persons. Each group is left alone in the room for a while during which time its members decide on a scene—historical, biblical, literary, etc.—which they represent as a tableau. The other players are then called in to guess the scene.

In the days when this game enjoyed great popularity, classical scenes and those borrowed from Shakespeare were the favorites. Today, subjects chosen for Tableaux Vivants might represent a dramatic moment from some television program or some popular contemporary personality. Here are a few alternative suggestions:

Florence Nightingale (lamp and wounded soldiers)
The Sleeping Beauty
Sir Francis Drake and Queen Elizabeth (cloak, etc.)
The three witches from *Macbeth*
Washington crossing the Delaware
Romeo and Juliet (balcony scene)
Snow White and the Seven Dwarfs
Three Wise Men with the Child Jesus

Acting Proverbs: This simple guessing game is suitable for small parties. Each player in turn fixes upon a proverb and acts it in pantomime before the others, whose task it is to guess the proverb represented. Props may be used.

The first player might, for instance, look at a watch or clock, lie down and feign sleep, wake up and consult the watch again and then, after standing up and stretching, throw out his chest to indicate health, count money to show wealth, and touch his forehead with his finger to demonstrate wisdom. ("Early to bed and early to rise maketh a man healthy, wealthy, and wise.") Other proverbs that can be acted include "A rolling stone gathers no moss," "There's many a slip 'twixt cup and lip," etc.

What Am I Doing?   This may be regarded as a sort of solo charade. One player stands in front of the rest of the party and goes through the motions of doing something—the more ludicrous, the better. Thus he may imitate the formidable task of washing down an elephant; he may pretend to do a jigsaw or catch a flea. The other players must try to guess his occupation, and if they are successful in doing so, the actor must pay a forfeit. This game is sometimes played with two principal actors, in which case they are allowed a minute or two of conspiracy to decide on their pretended task.

KISSING GAMES

Postman's Knock: This game can be used as a forfeit or played for its own sake. First of all, someone is stationed at the door *inside* the room to answer the knocks that will be made. Another person, the postman, goes outside the room and gives two knocks on the door. When the door is opened, the postman is asked for whom he has a letter and how many pennies the addressee must give for it. The recipient of the letter (a member of the opposite sex) must then go outside the room and pay the postman not in pennies but in kisses.

The Box of Secrets: This charming old game, which was very popular in France under the name of *la bôite d'amourette* ("the casket of passing fancy"), is simply a means of collecting forfeits—apart from the kissing, that is.

The player who starts the game presents a small box to his neighbor on the right, saying, "I will sell you my box of secrets; it contains three—whom I love, whom I will kiss, and whom I will send about his [or her] business." The neighbor, taking the box, must reply, "I will buy your box of secrets. Whom do you love? Whom will you kiss? Whom will you send about her business?" (We are assuming that in this instance the box seller is a gentleman.) The first speaker then names, in answer to the question, the lady in the company whom he loves, the one he intends to kiss (these must not be one and the same), and the one he intends to send about her business. The person to be kissed must submit to the operation on the spot, whereas the one sent about her business pays a forfeit. (No notice is taken of the loved one.) The buyer of the box must then sell it to the neighbor on her right.

Frincy-Francy: This game was never played in some parlors, for it was considered to lack refinement. But it was very popular at parties given in country farmhouses and was frequently played between dances.

A chair is placed in the middle of the room; the master of ceremonies leads to the chair a young lady who, sitting down, names the gentleman she wants to kiss her. He approaches her, kisses her, and then takes the seat himself. He then calls out the name of another lady, who is led to him by the master of ceremonies to receive her kiss. This lady then takes the seat, and so on until everyone has been well kissed. No sex equality here, be it noted: the gentlemen make their own way to the chair and its occupant, the ladies must be led!

The Drill Sergeant: The player chosen to be the drill sergeant selects any lady he chooses from the company and conducts her to the center of the room. Here he positions himself facing his troops who have fallen-in in front of him, with his lady standing a few inches behind him, also facing the troops. Like the sergeant, each soldier has a lady just behind him.

The sergeant now proceeds to drill the troops and in a stern voice gives the following words of command: "Attention!"—"Take ladies' hands!"—"Right about face!" —"Arms around waist!"—"Make ready!"—"Present!"— "Fire!" The last order is, of course, thoroughly understood even by the uninitiated, and each lady receives her amorous salute.

ROMP GAMES

Obstacle Race: Those who do not know the game are sent out of the room and brought back one by one. As each player enters, he is shown a number of obstacles placed in a line on the floor—an ornament or two, a footstool, a pile of books, etc. He is then blindfolded and told to walk over the obstacles without touching them, but before he starts his journey, the objects are quietly removed so that he walks carefully, stepping high to avoid what is no longer there.

Change: The players form a circle standing close together, and each is given an article to hold. All the articles must be different and of varying size and weight. A possible list is as follows:

   A walnut
   A book
   A cushion
   A bucket half full of water
   A frying pan
   An ashtray
   A carpet sweeper
   A suitcase
   A feather

On the word "Go," each player passes his object to the player on his right, who passes it on to the player on *his* right. This continues until the command "Change" is given by a nonplayer. At this, all the articles are passed in the opposite direction. To complicate the circular transit of the objects, two or three of them are designated always to be passed in the opposite direction to the rest. This, together with the need to handle successively light objects, heavy objects, large objects, and small objects is a great test of muscular coordination and is the cause of much confusion.

Any player who drops an object must retire from the circle, and the same for any player who is detected in passing, or trying to pass, an object in the wrong direction. The object concerned remains in the game, however, leaving the remaining players with a more difficult task. If all the players are eliminated except three or four, they will find themselves with armfuls of household articles of mixed character, and the exchanges become very difficult and complicated.

Quakers' Meeting: The company arrange themselves on the floor in a straight line, all kneeling on the right knee while on the other knee they rest their hands and twiddle their thumbs. It is forbidden to smile—any player detected doing so has to pay a forfeit. The following conversation is then carried on, each line of which must be repeated in turn by every player before the next line is said.

"Well friend, and how art thou?"
"Hast thou heard of Brother Obadiah's death?"
"No, how did he die?"
"With one finger up" (as each player repeats this line he stops twisting his thumbs and holds up his right forefinger),
"With one eye shut" (each closes his right eye),
"And shoulder all awry" (each does this).
"How did he die?"
"In this way."

At this point the player at the top of the row gives his neighbor a mighty shove, and the whole company goes over like a pack of cards.

Cutlets: This variation of Quakers' Meeting was immortalized by Charles Pooter in his *Diary of a Nobody* and cannot be better described than in his own words:

. . . as it was cold, we stayed in and played games; Gowing, as usual, overstepping the mark. He suggested we should play "Cutlets," a game we never heard of. He sat on a chair, and asked Carrie to sit on his lap, an invitation which dear Carrie rightly declined. After some species of wrangling, I sat on Gowing's knees and Carrie sat on the edge of mine. Lupin sat

on the edge of Carrie's lap, then Cummings on Lupin's, and Mrs. Cummings on her husband's. We looked very ridiculous and laughed a good deal. Gowing then said: "Are you a believer in the Great Mogul?" We had to answer all together: "Yes—oh, yes!" (three times). Gowing said: "So am I," and suddenly got up. The result of this stupid joke was that we all fell on the ground, and poor Carrie banged her head on the corner of the fender.

Rejected Addresses: This is a noisy game and a merry one. All the gentlemen leave the room, and the ladies arrange a row of chairs according to the number of men. Each of the absent gentlemen has a chair allocated to him, but no indication is given as to which chair belongs to which gentleman. A lady then takes up a place behind each chair, care being taken that no lady stands behind the chair allotted to her particular favorite.

The gentlemen are then called in, one by one. As each enters, all the ladies invite him to sit on her particular chair, each assuring him that he is the one allotted to it. Each lady will use all her feminine arts, charms, and wiles to tempt him into her chair. If the victim should be blandished into sitting in the wrong chair, all the ladies swoop upon him, pushing him, shoving him, and beating him with cushions until he is forced out of the room again. Should he be fortunate enough to choose the right chair, he is allowed to stay in the room and watch the fun.

Hiss and Clap: This is a more subdued version of the preceding game. After all the gentlemen have left the room, the ladies take their seats, each having a vacant space on her right-hand side for the gentleman of her choice. Each gentleman is summoned in turn and is asked which lady has chosen him for her partner. If he guesses correctly, he is clapped by the rest of the company and allowed to take his seat next to the lady who has chosen him; otherwise he is loudly hissed until he leaves the room.

The Knight of the Whistle: This game is only successful if a player can be found who does not know its secret. He is made the hunter. First he has to submit to the ceremony of conferring upon him the Knighthood of the Whistle. During this ceremony the whistle, which is on the end of a piece of string, is surreptitiously attached to the back of the hunter's coat with a bent pin.

He is then told to detect the player who has the whistle in his closed hand. None has, for the object of the game is for the other players to blow the whistle behind the hunter's back, and, of course, each time he turns around to locate it, it is again blown behind him. It generally takes the hunter a

considerable time to discover that the object of his search is
fastened to himself.

The Jolly Miller: A fairly large and unencumbered space is
required to play this game. Each gentleman chooses a lady
for a partner except the one who is to be the miller. He, the
solitary one, takes his place in the middle of the room while
his companions, arm in arm in couples, walk around him,
singing the following:

> *"There was a jolly miller who lived by himself.*
> *As the wheel went round, he made his wealth;*
> *One hand in the copper and the other in the bag,*
> *As the wheel went round he made his grab."*

At the word "grab," all the players must change partners
while the miller tries to secure a lady for himself; then,
needless to say, the unlucky gentleman without a partner
takes up the lonely position in the middle of the ring.

The Queen of Sheba: All the gentlemen are sent out of the
room. The ladies then select one of their number to play the
Queen, and the game proceeds thus. The first gentleman is
recalled, as though he himself were to undergo the ordeal of
"kissing the Queen of Sheba." In fact, the secret is explained
to him, and he joins the fair conspiracy, which is as follows.

All the ladies sit on the floor in two rows, facing each
other, their legs extended so that their feet just touch. At the
end of this lane and facing the door sits the "Queen of
Sheba" with a veil or shawl over her head. The second
gentleman is then brought in and told that if he can pass
through the lane of ladies *blindfolded* without stepping on any
limb, he will be allowed to kiss the Queen.

As soon as this player has been blindfolded, the Queen
gives up her position to the King (the first gentleman to have
entered the room), who assumes the throne and the veil and
sits awaiting the kiss. Meanwhile, all the ladies have drawn
in their feet to leave the path to the Queen unimpeded.
Unaware of this, the blindfolded player will perform the
most extraordinary acrobatics to reach the Queen and
deliver the kiss. He will probably receive some little guidance from the ladies on either side.

When he finally delivers the kiss, the blindfold is
removed to the delighted squeals of the Queen and her

Court. To allay the suspicions of the waiting gentlemen after the *first* of their number has been called in, it is a good idea for the ladies to simulate merriment after initiating the first gentleman into the secret of the game.

Feeding the Baby: Two volunteers are blindfolded and sit on the floor with knees touching. Each is given a bowl of broken biscuits, crumbled cake, or cornflakes, and a wooden spoon. A *wooden* spoon is essential if serious injuries are to be avoided. On the word "Go," each player endeavors to feed the other by filling his spoon and steering it into his partner's mouth. The spectacle is exceedingly funny.

Walking the Plank: A length of tape, about the size of the room, is laid upon the floor, and each person present has to walk its length while looking through a pair of binoculars or opera glasses the wrong way around. The contortions, poses, and facial expressions that result are quite extraordinary.

Crossing Niagara: A number of players are sent out of the room while the remainder prepare the scene as follows. A plank of wood some six feet long is suspended between two chairs. The first player is brought into the room and informed that he is to be blindfolded and hoisted onto the plank, which he must then walk. While he is undergoing the operation of being blindfolded, the plank is quietly taken from the chairs and laid on the floor. The blind man is then hoisted up by two other players and put down on the plank, which he will then walk much in the manner of Charles Blondin, who walked a tightrope across Niagara Falls.

Barnyard: One of the company goes around to the others, *supposedly* whispering the name of a farmyard animal to each. In fact, he tells them all to remain silent except one. This player is given "rooster," and on the command to the company for each person to imitate his animal, all together, all remain silent except for the solitary crowing of the rooster.

Topsy-Turvy Concert: This antic is so ridiculous that it is extremely funny. Some slight preparation is required before the game begins. The performers should be children of about the same height, and they should know the words of some catchy popular song that has both verse and chorus. "John Brown's Body" is a good example.

A sheet is stretched across the room, so that when the performers are standing behind it, only their heads can be seen by the rest of the party, who constitute the audience. Before starting the performance, the players place socks on their arms and shoes on their hands. (This is done in secrecy, behind the sheet.) At a given signal (and preferably with piano accompaniment), they all start singing.

During the verse ("John Brown's Body," etc.) they keep their hands and arms carefully hidden behind the sheet, but on the commencement of the chorus ("Glory, Glory Hallelujah") the singers quickly stoop down to hide their heads and thrust up their arms and hands, wildly waving them around to the music, the effect being that of a row of people singing while standing on their heads. At the beginning of the second verse the heads appear again, but each chorus is sung by the players apparently standing on their heads.

Brother, I'm Bobbed: Two chairs are placed side by side in the middle of the room and upon these chairs sit two blindfolded players, each supplied with a rolled-up newspaper. It is essential that one of the players knows the game while the other does not.

The player who knows the game removes his blindfold and hits himself on the head with his newspaper, saying, "Brother, I'm bobbed!" The other blindfolded player asks, "Brother, who bobbed you?" and the first player answers, pretending to guess one of the other players in the room.

He then hits his neighbor on the head, who in turn says, "Brother, I'm bobbed." "Brother, who bobbed you?" the first player asks. The second player then tries to guess the name of his assailant but never, of course, gets it right. The action is continued until the novelty wears off—a half a dozen bobs apiece is usually sufficient.

He Can Do Little Who Cannot Do This: This very simple game was a great favorite with Victorian children. Only those who know the secret escape paying a forfeit.

The first player (who must be in the know) takes a stick, umbrella, or broom in his hand and thumps it three or four times on the floor, afterward saying, "He can do little who cannot do this." He then passes the stick to the next player, who is supposed to do exactly the same on pain of forfeit.

The secret is that the first player thumps the stick with his left hand while subsequent players take it in their right.

Pillow Fight: Two players are blindfolded and given a pillow apiece. They are put into opposite corners of the room and told that a point will be awarded for every blow delivered to the enemy.

At this, they advance toward one another but, unknown to either of them, another player, *not blindfolded,* has also been furnished with a pillow, and he hits first one, then the other of the two blindfolded contestants, who meanwhile beat the empty air with their pillows and score very few points indeed.

Mirror Drawing: Each player is asked to draw an object, say a pig, on paper while looking through a mirror and not directly at the paper. A particularly difficult object to draw is a watch with its hand pointing to a definite time.

2

Word Games

*I*n this category, only games that require nothing more
than the power of speech for their performance are
included. Word games requiring any equipment,
such as a board, diagram, or even a pencil, are dealt
with in the following section (although in the case of
Proverbs and The Elements the use of a pocket handkerchief
is allowed). The advantages of word games are that they can
be played by any number of people without forethought or
preparation, at any time and in any place. "From thence to
the Hague," wrote Pepys, "again playing at Crambo in the
Wagon."

   The majority of the many word games played by the
Victorians would probably seem tedious to the modern
player. There was, for instance, Decapitations, a game in

which every player had to find a word which, when one of its end letters was removed, left another word that could be similarly decapitated, and so on (Abate, bate, ate, at, a).

Then there were Anagrams, Word Squares, and Enigmas—the latter game played around a chosen subject, as, for example, birds: Q. What does a sore throat prevent you from doing? A. Swallow. Q. Who was a famous architect? A. Wren. etc. Paragrams, Extractions, Definitions, Inversions, Metagrams, and Chronograms are also soporifics best omitted.

Most of the word games given here will be found suitable for play among mixed age groups and ideal for relieving the tedium of long journeys by road or rail.

Crambo: For some reason this game was the most popular of all Victorian parlor games. No party, adults' or children's, would have been complete without a few rounds of Crambo. The origin of the name of the game is not known.

One player leaves the room while the rest select a word. The guesser is then called in. He or she is told a word that rhymes with the chosen one and must go on to guess, *without naming them,* other words that rhyme with the chosen word until the latter is discovered. For example, let us suppose the chosen word is *play* and the clue given to the guesser is *hay.* The game might then continue as follows:

Q. Is it a month in Spring?
A. No, it is not May.
Q. Is it a path to somewhere?
A. No, it is not way.
Q. Is it the opposite to night?
A. No, it is not day.

And so on until the word is discovered.

Another version, known as Dumb Crambo, is played as follows. Half the company leaves the room while the other half decides on a word, which *must* be a verb. When the first team returns, the players are told another verb that rhymes with the one to be guessed.

Let's suppose the latter is *smell.* The guessers might be given *propel* as the clue and from that clue they must *act* the word they think to be the correct one. They might, for example, act the felling of a tree. Then, being wrong, they are hissed by their opponents. The procedure is continued until the right verb is discovered and acted.

Grandmother's Trunk: This is one of the oldest word games
on record. Each player has to repeat an ever-increasing list of
objects and to do so without so much as a smile. The first
player starts by saying, "My grandmother keeps an anchor in
her trunk" (or any article beginning with the letter A). The
player on his left must think of an article beginning with B,
such as "boot" and say, "My grandmother keeps anchors and
boots in her trunk."

Thus the game continues, each player having to remember all the odds and ends kept in his grandmother's
trunk and to try to add one so ridiculous that it will make one
of his fellow players smile or laugh. This disqualifies him, as
does an inability to remember the full list of Grandmother's
possessions.

The Traveler's Alphabet: The first player says, "I am going
to Amsterdam" (or any other place beginning with A). The
player on his left then asks, "What will you do there?" and he
must be answered with a sentence in which the verb,
adjective, and noun begin with the letter A.

The second player now announces his departure for
Belgium or any place beginning with a B and is likewise
questioned. The game goes like this.

Player 1.   I am going to Amsterdam.
Player 2.   What will you do there?
Player 1.   I shall artfully avoid anchovies.

Player 2.   I am going to Belgium.
Player 3.   What will you do there?
Player 2.   I shall bury bullocks' bones.
Player 3.   I am going to Canada.
Player 4.   What will you do there?
Player 3.   I shall catch a craven coward.

And so on until X, Y, and Z are dealt with or another game is called for. Forfeits for failures and mistakes, of course.

Ship's Alphabet: A captain is elected, and the rest of the players sit in front of him. The captain points to the first player and asks, "The name of the letter?" The name of the letter *must* be A, and all the questions must be answered with a word beginning with A. The next letter must be B, and so forth.

Captain: The name of the letter?
Player 1:   A
Captain: The name of the ship?
Player 2:   Alec
Captain: The name of the captain?
Player 3:   Arthur
Captain: The name of the cargo?
Player 4:   Apples
Captain: The port she came from?
Player 5:   Amsterdam
Captain: The place she is bound for?
Player 6:   Agra
Captain: The name of the letter?
Player 1:   B, etc.

All answers must be given before the captain can count to ten, and failures or mistakes involve forfeits.

The Minister's Cat: Any number can play this game, and the more the merrier. The first player describes the minister's cat with any adjective beginning with the letter A. For instance, "The minister's cat is an angry cat." The next player must also use an A. "The minister's cat is an amiable cat." This continues for one round, at which the letter B is taken and so on throughout the alphabet. Players drop out if they are unable to find an adjective or if they repeat one already used. The game *can* get past X, for see "xenial," "Xeresian," or "xenophobic" as only three examples.

I Love My Love: This very old game can be played by any number of players. The players merely have to answer a number of questions with epithets, all of which must begin with the same letter, as in this example:

Q. Why do you love your love?
A. Because he is amiable.
Q. Why do you hate your love?
A. Because he is argumentative.
Q. Where did you meet your love?
A. At the sign of the Angel.
Q. What did he feed you there?
A. He fed me on asparagus.
Q. What is the name of your love?
A. His name is Archibald.
Q. Where does your love live?
A. He lives at Andover.

When one player has gotten this far, the questioning passes to the next, who has to answer with words beginning with the letter B. The game goes on throughout the alphabet, with the exclusion of X and Z. Players are out if they cannot answer a question correctly and at once or if, during a second time around, they repeat an answer already used.

I Love My Love (a simpler version):
The profession of love is simplified as follows:

A   I love my love with an A, because he is affectionate, because his name is Augustus. I will give him an amethyst, feed him on apple tart, and make him a bouquet of anemones.
B   I love my love with a B, because she is beautiful, because her name is Beatrice. I will give her a brooch, feed her on black currants, and make her a bouquet of bluebells.

Forbidden Letters: A letter of the alphabet is chosen, and the players are forbidden to use it in any word when answering the selected questioner. Furthermore a player must not answer with the words "yes" or "no." If, for example, the forbidden letter is E and the question is "Do you like this game?," the answer cannot be "yes," "no," "I like it" or any other reply containing an E. His reply *could* be

"Not much" or "A bit." If a player answers wrongly, he is out.

Flour Merchant: The player taking the part of the flour merchant must try to sell his stock of flour by asking questions of the other players one by one. The others must resist his salesmanship but without using the words "flour," "I," "yes," or "no." Any player caught using one of these words must pay a forfeit.

> *Flour Merchant:* Do you want some flour today?
> *Player:* None is required.
> *Flour Merchant:* Let me persuade you to take a sample.
> *Player:* Impossible.
> *Flour Merchant:* Why?
> *Player:* You heard my answer.
> *Flour Merchant:* Then I must have forgotten it. What was it?
> *Player:* I won't take any.

The flour merchant, having succeeded in obtaining an "I," goes on to the next player.

Proverbs (1): The players sit in a circle. One has a rolled-up handkerchief or a ball of paper which he suddenly throws at one of the players. The others now count up to ten in unison, and before they finish the person hit must quote a proverb. Proverbs must not be repeated, and any player who fails to speak in time must retire or pay a forfeit.

Proverbs (2): One of the company is sent out of the room. The others decide on a proverb, a well-known quotation, or any known expression, to be discovered by him on his return. To effect the discovery, he is entitled to ask questions from the company all around, beginning with the player on his left.

He may ask any question he pleases, but the answer must contain the first word of the proverb, the answer to the second question must contain the second word, and so forth, each member of the party taking a word in succession, and the questions going around the company as many times as is necessary until the proverb is completed.

The great difficulty in this game is to contrive answers in such a way that the fatal word is not conspicuous. It is best to choose proverbs or quotations composed of the most common words, such as "Many hands make light work," and *not* those that give themselves away like "Too many cooks spoil the broth." If, for instance, the chosen proverb was "Procrastination is the thief of time," the game would not survive the first word.

Shouting Proverbs: As in the previous game, one player leaves the room while the others agree on a proverb. One word of the proverb is given to each of the company, any players being left over having to stand down for this round of the game. The guesser then returns, stands in front of the other players, and orders, "Load! Aim! FIRE!" At the word "fire," they all shout out their particular words together, and from the resulting noise he is expected to guess the proverb. He is allowed three attempts.

Quotations: One person, usually the host, quotes half a quotation to the first guest in the line and asks him to complete it. It is best, of course, to write down a number of familiar quotations in preparation for this game. Thus:

> "All that glitters . . . is not gold."
> "Give me liberty or . . . give me death."
> "Come into the garden, Maud . . . For the black bat,
>   night, has flown."

Poet's Chair: The Poet's Chair is set in the middle of the room and the players sit around it. The first poet takes the chair and recites any line of poetry, or, if preferred, a couplet.

> *"You are old, Father William," the young man cried,*
>   *"The few locks that are left you are gray."*

The players must now try to think of a line of poetry beginning with the letter G—that is, the initial letter of the last word of the last quotation. The first to do so claims the Poet's Chair.

> *"Green grow the rushes, O."*

The next line must begin with an O:

> *"Onward, Christian soldiers."*

No line may be used more than once, and there is no scoring.

Endless Story: The participants sit in a circle and one of them starts off a story—any story at all. He may continue for up to a minute and then, without finishing the story, he touches the person on his right, who must continue the narrative, even from the middle of a sentence. This continues until the chain reaches the person who started it, and he must bring it to a successful conclusion—also within a minute.

One Syllable: The company should be seated in a circle, ladies and gentlemen alternately. A lady begins by asking a question of the player on her right, to which he must reply in one word of one syllable or incur a forfeit for every extra syllable. Played at a party in the nineteenth century, the conversation might have gone as follows:

Lady: Permit me, sir, to ask if you love music.
Gent: Yes. (Then, to the lady on his right.) Pray, madam, what wood do you think best for making loggerheads?
Lady: Oak. Pray, sir, who is the cleverest man in the world?
Gent: I. What kind of people prosper most in the world?
Lady: Fools. Pray, sir, are you not romantic?
Gent: Yes, But who is handsomest, you or I?
Lady: I. What sort of girl do you think I am?
Gent: Mad. Which do you prefer, champagne or claret?
Lady: Claret. (She pays a forfeit).

I've Been to Market: The company forms into a circle, and one of the players says to his neighbor on the left, "I've been to market." The neighbor inquires, "What have you bought?" The first player may then name any article that comes into his head, provided that he is able, on saying the word, to *touch* an article such as he has named. This may be an article on his own person, such as a coat, a shoe, a pen, etc., or something within his reach such as a carpet, a dress, a brooch, a chair, etc. Whoever is unable to name an article not previously indicated is punished by paying a forfeit.

The Elements: The players sit around in a circle, and one of them throws a screwed-up handkerchief to another, calling at the same time "earth" (or "air" or "water") and then counting, quite rapidly, up to ten. The player to whom the handkerchief is thrown must give the name of some animal that lives on earth (if "air" is called, some bird, or if "water" is called, some fish) before the thrower has counted to ten. If he fails, he pays a forfeit, but either way he throws the handkerchief at someone else, and so on.

Proper Names: One player leaves the room while the rest agree on a proper noun. When he comes back, he must ask each person in turn a question in an effort to find out the chosen name. The questions are put as in the game of Twenty Questions, but the answers must always be formed in this way (as in Crambo): "No, it is not . . . " or "Yes, but it's not . . . " The missing word must *always* begin with the same letter as the chosen word, and the answer must always be true. Supposing the chosen word is Beethoven, then the dialogue might go like this:

Q. Is it a city in England?
A. No, it is not Birmingham.
Q. Is it a man?
A. Yes, but it's not Bunyan.
Q. Is he alive?
A. No, it is not Bernstein.
Q. Is he a musician?
A. Yes, but it's not Bach.
     etc.

Anyone failing to answer correctly is declared out. The questioner wins if he gets the answer within an agreed time limit, or within a given number of questions. Otherwise he pays a forfeit.

Ghosts: Any number of players can play Ghosts. Each is allowed five lives; when he has lost all five, he is out of the game. The first player says a letter, the next adds a letter, the next a third letter and so on. The object of the game is to *avoid* completing a word—the player who does so loses a life, as does a player who cannot add a letter that leads to a word.

> *Player 1:*   D
> *Player 2:*   DE
> *Player 3:*   DEC
> *Player 4:*   DECO (He must avoid DECK, for this loses him a life.)
> *Player 5:*   DECOR (a foreign word, so allowable)
> *Player 6:*   DECORO
> *Player 7:*   DECOROU
> *Player 8:*   DECOROUS (He has no choice and so loses a life.)

If, for example, Player 7 thinks that there is no word beginning with DECORO he may challenge Player 6, and if Player 6 supplies that word, Player 7 loses a life. If Player 6 cannot give the word, he loses a life. The next player after the one who loses a life now starts with another letter, and the game continues until only one player remains alive.

3

Table Games

*A*ll the games described in the previous chapter can, of course, be played across a table—indeed many are better for it. In this section, however, we include games which, whether or not they require special equipment, are more comfortably played over a table than on the floor.

Games needing no special equipment are, in the main, word games that require only a pencil and paper. The most famous of them is the game of Consequences, which was already well established in the sixteenth century. It is described by Ben Johnson in *Cynthia's Revels:*

> Why, I imagine a thing done; Hedon thinks who did it;

Maria with what it was done; Anaides, where it was done; Argurion, when it was done; Amorphus, for what cause it was done; you, Philantia, what followed upon the doing of it; and this gentleman, who would have done it better.

The game has continued to be popular up to the present century and was a great favorite in the Victorian parlor.

Hundreds of different board games were played in Victorian parlors, but most of them were played with special boards and pieces which no longer exist, so we have confined our selection to those that can be played on available or easily made-up boards. Chess and backgammon have been excluded, as these games have their own special bibliographies.

Board games have been played for thousands of years, as is evidenced by drawings found on the walls of Egyptian tombs some five thousand years old. Sets of the Egyptian game of Senet (also known to the ancients as Thirty Squares) have been found intact, for no Egyptian king was buried without a set of this game with which to help while away eternity. A set of Senet comprised a board on which were marked three lines of ten squares each, and a number of pawnlike pieces. The method of playing the game is not known, but it is probable that it was similar to that of our backgammon. Another game that was very similar to backgammon was the ancient Roman game of *Duodecim scripta*, which was played on a board marked with twelve double lines.

Games of the checkers family have been played since prehistoric times and have even found their way into legend, for Athena found the suitors of Penelope seated on cowhides playing a form of checkers. The earliest form of the game was played by two players with five pieces each on a board marked with five lines. The lines were added to over the years until they numbered eleven, and later still these lines developed into the board of squares we use today.

A game similar to checkers, which developed independently from the European game, is the African Mancala, a game that is played under different names and with slightly differing rules by Bantu, Nilotes, Hamites, and Semites all over the African continent. So involved is the play and so complicated are the rules of Mancala that it is rare for a European to master the game.

Even the very Victorian game of Ludo (it was patented and commercialized in the 1890's) has an ancient history, and, indeed, a very glamorous one, for it is a descendant of the Hindu game of Parcheesi, invented by one of the old Mogul emperors. He played it on a courtyard paved in the design of a board and used slave girls as pieces.

The game of dominoes is believed to have been invented in China during the eleventh century; some sources say it goes back to around A. D. 200. It seems to have been unknown in Europe until the 1700's, when it appeared in Italy, where it was named from the ebony backing of each tile, which was said to resemble the cloak known as a domino. Of the twelve varieties of Dominoes, the standard or "block" game and four other forms that were popular in earlier days are included here.

Finally, I have included the "solo" board game of Solitaire (not to be confused with the card game of the same name) because it is now enjoying a deserved revival. A set of Solitaire looks attractive even in the most modern parlor, and, needing no setting up, it is always handy to provide something to do in idle or waiting moments. With its pretty glass pieces and the satisfying clicking as one by one they are removed, the game provides a calming and relaxing entertainment.

PENCIL-AND-PAPER GAMES

Consequences: (oral):   This delightful old game was a parlor favorite until comparatively recently. Any number of players can take part, each one being supplied with a sheet of notepaper and a pencil. Each player writes down on the top of his paper one or more adjectives that can be applied to human beings—"fat," "happy," "brilliant," "ugly," "ambitious," etc. He then folds the top of the paper in such a way as to conceal what he has written. Each then passes his paper to the player on his left, who writes upon it the name of a man—either one of the company or some celebrity. The papers are again folded and passed to the left, the procedure continuing as follows:

3. Who the man met (this must be a woman)

4. Where they met
5. What he gave her
6. What he said to her
7. What she replied
8. What the consequence was
9. What the world said

The papers are then opened, and the resulting episodes are read aloud.

There is a longer version of this game in which the sequence is as follows:

Adjective describing a man
The man's name
What he was wearing
What he was doing at the time

met

Adjective describing the lady
The lady's name
What she was wearing
What she was doing
The person she would much rather have met
Where the meeting took place
What he thought
What he said
What she thought
What she said
Where they went
What they did there
The consequence
What the world said

Celebrities: In this game a leader is chosen, and all the other players are supplied with pencil and paper. The leader then announces a letter of the alphabet—in this case let us say B. The players then have three minutes in which to write down all the celebrities they can think of whose names begin with B. They may be actors, businessmen, writers, musicians, murderers, statesmen, etc. In case of dispute the leader is the final judge as to whether or not a person is a celebrity.

At the end of the three minutes, each player reads his list aloud. One point is allowed for every name that does not appear on any other list. If, therefore, the first player announces Beethoven, then all other players cross Beethoven off their lists. The player with the highest score wins. The art of the game is to choose lesser-known celebrities. For instance, Bartok, Bradshaw, Beaumont, and Belloc stand a much higher chance of scoring than do Beethoven, Browning, Beecham, and Brahms.

Doublets: This puzzle game was invented by Lewis Carroll in 1879. The rules of the game are simple, the playing of it is not. Two words are taken, each containing the same number of letters, and these words are joined by "links" forming them into phrases or sentences. Thus "Drive PIG into STY." The object of the game is to change the word PIG into the word STY by changing one letter at a time, but through a chain of real words, thus:

    PIG
    pit
    sit
    sat
    say
    STY

The player who completes the transposition with the smallest number of changes wins that round and is awarded with the same number of points as there are letters in the two key words. In the above example, six points would be given. Other examples are these:

    Prove a ROGUE to be a BEAST
    ROGUE
    vogue
    vague
    value
    valve
    halve
    helve
    heave
    leave
    lease
    least
    BEAST

Try some of the following:

Raise FOUR to FIVE.
Make WHEAT into BREAD.
Dip PEN into INK.
Touch CHIN with NOSE.
Change TEARS into SMILE.
PITCH TENTS.
Cover EYE with LID.
Prove PITY to be GOOD.
Make EEL into PIE.
Evolve MAN from APE.
Make FLOUR into BREAD.
Get COAL from MINE.

Square Words: A word is selected, its length being a matter of taste, for the longer the word, the more difficult the game. Let us suppose it to be PASTIME. Each player writes this word on a piece of paper downward on one side, upward on the other.

```
P           E
A           M
S           I
T           T
I           S
M           A
E           P
```

The players then have to supply letters to form words that begin and end with the letters as they stand. A fixed time is allowed for this, say five minutes, and at the end of this time each player calls out his words. The words should be as unusual as possible, since a word formed by more than one player does not score. Words of less than four letters are not allowed.

The longer the word chosen, the more difficult becomes the game, for in a long word there is more chance of the vowels falling together, and the combinations of such vowels as A and U or their reverse are difficult to fit into a word, especially if proper nouns are ruled out.

A possible solution to the square given above might be this:

```
P a s t E
A l a r M
S p a g h e t t I
```

T a i n T
I l l n e s S
M e m o r a n d A
E n w r a P

Gallows or *Hangman:*   This ever-popular game can be
enjoyed by any number of persons, irrespective of age. One
player, the hangman, chooses a word (any word), announces
how many letters it contains, and marks on a piece of paper
the same number of blanks. Suppose the word to be
"Capricorn" (nine letters), the nine blanks are indicated
thus _ _ _ _ _ _ _ _ _.

The condemned man (or men), desperately seeking
reprieve, asks the hangman whether the word contains any
E's. The answer, in this case, is "no," and the hangman starts
to build his gallows. Asked next if there are any C's, the
hangman is compelled to place the C's on the first and sixth
blanks, where they belong, and he must postpone the
erection of his gallows.

The game continues in this manner until the Condemned Man either wins a reprieve by discovering the word
before the gallows is built and the hanging takes place, or
until the execution is carried out. The sequence of gallows
construction and the "turning off" is effected as follows.

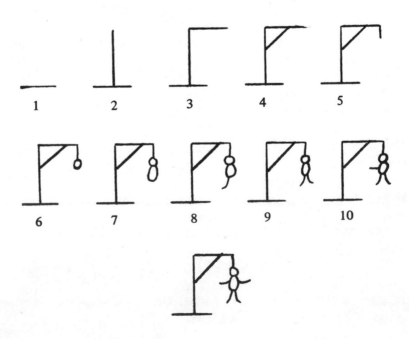

More often than not, the longer the word, the easier it will be for the condemned to obtain a reprieve, and even a simple word like "wry" will usually cost a man his neck. Obscure words are not barred, although technical ones usually are. The game is sometimes played by reducing the number of guesses to eight. This is done by omitting the horizontal line on which the gallows stands and assuming that the condemned man has no arms.

Squares or *Boxes:*   A development of Ticktacktoe, Squares may be played by two, three, or four players. Lines of dots are set out in a square, the size of the square depending upon the length of time desired to play the game.

It will be seen that the large square contains a number of potential small squares that can be made by joining the dots together horizontally or vertically. The players take turns making these joins with the object of obtaining as many of these squares as possible, the square going to the player who adds the completing stroke.

The game opens with a selected player drawing a stroke from one dot to another. Each does this in turn, endeavoring to place his stroke in a way that will make it impossible for the next player to complete a square. At first this is simple enough, but there comes a point in the game when a player has no choice but to put in the third stroke to a square and leave it for his successor to complete.

The player finishing a square writes his initials within it to prove ownership and is allowed another stroke. It will be seen that in completing the first square, the player may well open up the opportunity of completing another—and yet another. It is therefore necessary for the previous player to think very carefully in order to keep down that number.

Original Sketches: Each player is supplied with a pencil and paper, at the top of which a small sketch is drawn by everyone. The sketch may represent some historical incident, a proverb, or any other subject chosen.

When all the sketches are completed, each player passes his picture to his left-hand neighbor, who examines the picture and writes on the *bottom* of the paper what he thinks its meaning to be. He then folds the paper so as to conceal the writing and passes it to the player on *his* left. He, in turn, writes down his interpretation but without looking at what has already been written.

As soon as the sketches have been examined and commented on by all the players, they are collected, the papers unfolded, and the various opinions read aloud.

The Maze: This is a game for two players. A number of dots or small circles are marked out in the form of a square. The first player marks two of the dots and his opponent has to connect them with a line—it need not be the most direct one. The second player then marks two dots and the first player must connect them. The game is easy enough at the beginning but becomes increasingly complex because neither player must touch any unmarked dot or cross or touch any of the lines. Each time a player does so, he loses a mark.

Up Jenkins: Another very old game. Two sides, each with a captain, seat themselves on either side of a long table. One team possesses a small coin, which they pass from hand to hand under cover of the table. As soon as he thinks that sufficient time has been given to hide the coin, the captain of the other side calls, "Up Jenkins," and all the closed fists of the coin-holding side are held above the table. The captain then calls, "Down Jenkins," at which the hands are brought down upon the table palms downward. This movement is made as loudly as possible so as to drown the chink of the coin as it strikes the table.

The coinless team members then put their heads together to try to decide whose hand the coin is *not* under, asking each of the opposing side in turn to show their hands. A clever team will be able to guess with some success by studying the faces and demeanor of the members of the opposing party. Should a mistake be made and a hand called up under which the coin *was* hidden, the coin remains with the same side for the next round. If the last hand left on the counter covers the coin, it passes to the guessing side. The side that first scores ten points wins the game.

BOARD GAMES

Checkers: This game is for two players and is played on a board of 64 squares, 32 black and 32 white (or red). The board is placed so that each player has a black square at his right-hand lower corner. There are 24 pieces, or "men," 12 of each color. The men are laid out on the white (or red) squares of the first three rows on each side of the board. The pieces move diagonally from square to square either to the left or right. They may never move across or straight back or forward. Each player moves forward one square at a time, in turn. Players draw for color, and black starts.

One piece takes another by jumping over the opposing man into a vacant square—the man taken is removed from the board. Any number of men can be taken in this way in a move.

As soon as a man arrives at any of the four squares in the last opposite row, he is crowned and becomes a king (another man is placed on top of the advanced piece). The king has the privilege of moving either backward or forward, but only one square at a time. The object of the game is to capture the enemy's men, or to block them in such a way that they cannot move; the player who first accomplishes either of these objects wins.

Fox and Geese: This is a game for two players using a checkers board and five men—four white and one black. It is an exciting game requiring some skill but with the drawback that if the player manipulating the four geese (the white pieces) knows the secret, the fox (played by the black piece) cannot possibly elude them.

The object of the game is for the geese to force the fox into a corner while the fox tries to elude them and get through to the opposite side of the board. The geese are placed on the four white squares on the side of the board next to the player who is playing them; the fox is placed by *its* player on any white square of his choice.

The moves are the same as in checkers—that is, diagonally. The geese are allowed to move forward only, whereas the fox can move both back and forth. There is no "jumping" over pieces and no taking. The geese are entitled to the first move, after which the moves are taken alternately. As long as the geese keep as far as possible in a straight line, making their forward movements at points farthest from the fox, the latter will not be able to break through, but much practice on the part of the geese is required before the secret of winning is mastered.

Go Bang: This game was the Victorian adaptation of the Japanese game of Go and was, in fact, played with identical

equipment. For those who cannot quite grasp the immensities involved in the Oriental game, Go Bang is a simple substitute.

It is played by two or four persons on a flat board divided into four hundred squares, twenty by twenty. To each of two players are allocated two hundred pieces of distinctive color, or one hundred each to four players. The players set down a piece of any one of the unoccupied squares on any part of the board, and the game is won by the first player to get five of his men together in a straight or diagonal line. A patented version of this game using a holed board and pegs for pieces was once available under the name of Peggity.

Checkers Go Bang: This version of Go Bang is played by two people on a checkers board with an ordinary set of pieces. Each player alternately places one of his pieces on *any* vacant square on the board until all the pieces are in place. If during this operation either player succeeds in getting five of his men in a line, vertically, horizontally, or diagonally, he wins the game. This, however, rarely happens.

Once all the pieces are on the board, each player alternately moves one of his pieces to any adjoining square with the object of forming a line of five of his men. Whichever player first succeeds in doing this says, "Go Bang" and is the winner.

Losing Checkers: This is not a difficult game, and although it cannot be said to be quite so interesting as the regular game, it is full of variety and makes a change from the original. The point of the game is for the player to bring up his men in a manner not only to force his opponent to take as many pieces as possible in one move, but also to arrange his own men to keep up a succession of losing hazards.

It is, of course, possible for a player with half a dozen men left on the board to compel his opponent to take them all with a single king; or, easier still, for a single king to move in such a way as to compel his adversary to give up his men one by one until he, the king, finds a way of committing suicide. Otherwise the rules of the game are exactly the same as those for regular checkers.

Nine Men's Morris (2 players):   This very ancient game was at one time played with stones as "men" on a diagram marked out on the ground, usually outside the village inn or on the green. The game was once known as Fippeny Morrell.

Nine Men's Morris boards can still be bought but can be just as easily drawn on paper. Two persons play, each having nine men or counters. Each player puts down a man alternately, one by one, upon the spots at the points of intersection of the lines, the object being to prevent the opponent from placing three of his pieces as to form a row. If a row is formed, the player who made it takes off one of his competitor's pieces from whatever part of the board he chooses, but *not* from any row of three *unless* there is no other piece to remove.

When all nine men of both sides have been played, the players move those that are left backward and forward in any direction in which the lines run, but only to an adjoining spot. In this way they continue to try to form "threes" and

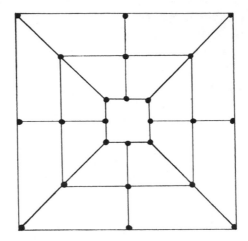

still remove an opposing piece when they succeed in doing so. The player who takes off all his opponent's pieces wins the game.

French and English: A piece of paper about eighteen inches by twelve is marked out as the battlefield.

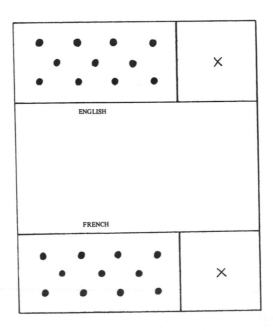

The players decide the order of play, and the first (let us say he is English) puts the point of a pencil on the "cannon" (marked with a cross) on the English side. He then closes his eyes, turns away his head and "fires" at the enemy by drawing

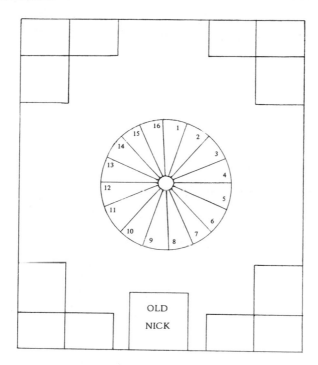

the pencil rapidly toward the other side. The pencil will leave a line, and all men on the other side through which this line passes count as slain.

The track of the pencil may be straight or curved but any track containing an angle does not count. The players play alternately, and the winner is he who first kills all the men on the other side.

Tit-Tat-Toe (not to be confused with Ticktacktoe): Several people can join this old table game, which in Georgian and Victorian times used to be played on a slate. It can now be just as well played with pencil and paper. A circle is drawn and divided into as many divisions as is thought necessary, sixteen generally being the least (*see* illustration on this page). The divisions are numbered, the center containing a higher number than any in the divisions, usually 25 or 50.

Each player has a square on which to record the numbers he obtains. A space on the board is allotted to Old Nick. The players alternately take a pencil in their hand, holding it point down on division 1. They then shut their eyes and tap the pencil around the ring, making one tap for each word of the following rhyme, which they recite aloud.

"Tit, tat, toe, my first go,
Three jolly butcher boys all in a row.
Stick one up, stick one down,
Stick one in the old man's ground."

On the last word they keep the pencil where it has fallen, open their eyes and record, each in his own square, the number at which the pencil stopped. This number is now crossed out on the diagram to signify that it is taken and the other players proceed in the same manner.

The process is repeated until all the numbers have been taken, or until one puts his pencil in the center ring. The scores are then added up, the highest being the winner. If all the figures are taken before the center is touched, the game goes to Old Nick. If one player puts his pencil in a division already taken, he records nothing and loses that turn; this is also the case if, on the last word of the verse, the pencil is found to be on a line or outside the circle.

Coronet: This game is played by six players on a board which is simple to draw (*see* below). It should be made large enough for each of the six compartments to contain eight counters, which may bear a real or nominal value. The game can, of course, also be played with coins.

Each player chooses a compartment of the circle and deposits eight counters therein. The player who has the 6-compartment throws a die; the others throw in rotation

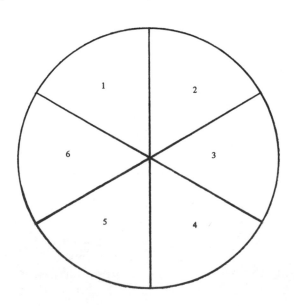

and whatever number is thrown, the owner of that compartment receives four counters (or coins)—two from the compartment on his left, and two from that on his right.

Should one of the players lose all the eight counters staked before the end of the game, he may, if he wishes, stake eight fresh counters, and the game proceeds as before. If, on the other hand, he decides not to stake further counters, then any other player may claim that compartment by staking eight counters upon it. Should no one occupy a compartment, it is considered nonexistent, and if its number should come up, the die is cast again. In the event of a blank compartment, the players receive winnings from the nearest right- or left-hand compartment.

The game is won by the player who first increases his eight counters to eighteen or more, and as the winner, he receives one counter from each player.

DOMINO GAMES

Dominoes are little flat tiles of wood, bone, ivory, or (in today's form) plastic. The face of each tile forms a double square, and each square, except those that are left blank, bears a number of dots, known as pips, ranging from one to six. The full set consists of twenty-eight tiles, ranging from double-six to double-blank.

It will be seen that the set consists, in various combinations, of eight blanks, eight ones (or aces), eight twos (or deuces), eight threes (or trays), eight fours, fives and sixes—every number, therefore, being equally represented. In naming a given domino, the higher number is always mentioned first, as six-five, tray-deuce, deuce-ace, etc.

The principle of most domino games is the placing or posing of tiles by each player alternately, so as to "follow suit"—that is, in such manner that one end of the card last placed must correspond in number with the *outer* end of one of those already on the table, the corresponding numbers being placed in juxtaposition.

The shuffling of the tiles is common to all domino games. This is done by turning them facedown on the table and mixing them up with the fingers. Each player has the right to join in this operation. The right to first *pose* (that is, to lay down the first tile) is then decided by each player turning up one domino; the drawer of the lowest number of

pips wins preference. The dominoes thus used are returned
to the pack, which is then reshuffled. Each player then draws
at random from the pack until he has in hand the number
appropriate to the game to be played.

The Block Game: This is the parent of all domino games,
for two players. Each player draws seven tiles. The leader
(A) poses face upward any tile he pleases—for example, the
six-five. His opponent (B) must play to this a second tile,
also having at one of its ends either a six or a five—the six or
five end must be placed touching the corresponding end of
the tile already played.

A must now play either a five or a three. We will
suppose that he plays double-five. (It is usual to place a
double crosswise to the line.) This does not alter the
position, and B in turn can only play a tile that has a five or a
three. He plays, say, five-four, which he places against A's
double. A continues with, say, four-ace, and B (at the
opposite end) with three-four.

It is now A's turn, and we will suppose that he has
neither a four nor an ace. He is consequently "blocked," and
B plays again. If he can maintain the block, he will do so,
and we will suppose that he does so by playing double-four,
leaving A still unable to play. B continues with three-ace. A
responds with three-five and B with five-ace.

Now we will suppose that neither player has a four or an
ace left. Both are therefore "blocked," and the hand is at an
end. The players add together the total pips they still hold
unplayed, and whoever has the lowest number wins. This is
the simplest way of scoring, and when it is used a rubber of
three games is usually played.

Sometimes the game is played for a given number, say
50, 60, or 100. In this case the holder of the smaller number
scores the *difference* of points between himself and his
adversary—that is, if A has twelve pips left in his hand and B
seven, the latter scores five toward game. When one player
scores "domino" (gets rid of all his tiles), he scores the whole
number of points left in the hand of his adversary.

Sebastopol or *The Fortress:*   This is a four-handed version of
the Block Game, each combatant playing independently.
All the dominoes are divided, and the holder of the
double-six leads, playing that tile. Each player in rotation
must play a six or pass. The first and second six played are

placed above and below the double, the other two at right angles to it, forming a cross. After the first round, a player may play to any number that is open, and the game proceeds as in the Block Game.

Matadors: The two players each draw seven tiles, and the one who has the highest double begins. The object in this case is not to *match* the end number, but to play to it such a number as, added to it, will make seven. Thus if a five has been laid down, then a two must be played; if a four, a three; if a six, an ace; and so on. If the player whose turn it is cannot make seven, he is blocked, and must draw from the reserve until he gets a tile that will allow him to play.

Since six is the highest point, a blank would create an absolute block. To prevent such a block, four dominoes, the six-ace, the five-two, the four-three (that is, all those which in themselves make seven) and the double blank are known as matadors, and may not only be played to a blank but to any number whatsoever. If a player is blocked, he must continue to draw until he can play, subject to the rule that at least two dominoes must be left undrawn.

Although a matador may be played to any number, the converse does not hold. The opposing player can only follow a matador with a tile making seven when added to one of the ends of the matador. Thus to a six-ace a player must play either a one or a six, to a five-deuce, either a two or a five, and so on.

Sometimes matadors are placed crosswise at the end of the line, and it is left open to the adversary to play to either end of it, as he pleases; the more usual practice is to allow the player of a matador to place it as he thinks best, in which case his opponent can play only to the exposed end. Let us suppose that A (the leader) plays a double-six, and B replies with ace-blank. A, if he plays to the blank, must do so with a matador. He plays, say, five-two. He may place it either as shown on page 90 in Figure 1 or in Figure 2. B, in the first case, must now play either an ace or a five; in the second case, an ace or a two.

It is customary, although not compulsory, to place a matador at right angles to the rest of the line, as shown in the figures.

In play a double counts only as a single piece. Thus double-six is merely regarded as six, and an ace must be played to it. But in reckoning up the score, which is done on the same principle as in the Block Game, the full number of pips is counted. Should the game become blocked while one of the players still holds a matador, he can, of course, open it, but he is not bound to do so if he considers that it is in his interest for the game to end at that point.

Blanks are very useful in this game, as only matadors can be played to them. The play of a blank, therefore, will either leave the adversary blocked, or compel him to part with a matador. It is, on the other hand, unsafe to play a blank unless the player himself has one or more matadors in his hand, for otherwise the blank may operate to his disadvantage.

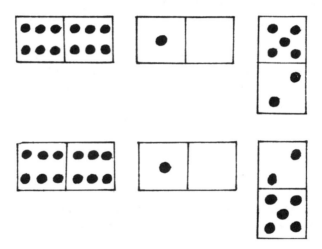

Domino Loo (3 or 4 players):   This is a version of the card game of the same name but played with dominoes. We suggest that those who are unfamiliar with the card game should look at the description given on page 110 before attempting to play Domino Loo.

The game is best played by three or four players, each playing five dominoes and each putting up a stake, the amount of which is divisible by five. The dealer puts up a double stake. The tiles are regarded as of six different suits—the six suit, the five suit, and so on down to the ace suit. The player of any given tile has the right to decide to which of the two suits it shall be considered to belong.

The tiles are shuffled, and the dealer gives five to each player. As in the card game, he also deals an extra hand known as "miss." He then turns up one tile from the stock to decide trumps. This is governed by the *heavier* end of the turned-up tile. Thus, if six-three is turned up, sixes will be the trump suit. If a double is turned up, then that number will be trumps.

Any player dissatisfied with his hand (beginning with the elder hand, that is, the one on the left of the dealer) has, in turn, the option of taking "miss"—that is, he takes up the extra hand in place of his own, which he discards. The dealer has the right to take the turned-up (trump) tile into his hand, discarding (without showing) any tile from his hand.

The elder hand now leads, placing the tile face upward on the table, and at the same time naming it. The order in which he names the point determines the suit to which he wishes it to belong. Thus, if he plays five-four, and so announces it, the tile belongs to the five suit, but if he calls it four-five it belongs to the four suit.

The other players must follow suit, if able, and the highest wins the trick. If a player cannot follow suit, he may trump—that is, play a tile of the trump suit, or he may discard a tile of any other suit. A player is not bound to head the trick (win it), or to trump it, but if he holds two trumps, he is bound to play one of them; and, after winning a trick, he is bound to lead a trump if able to do so.

At the end of the game, each trick won entitles the player to a fifth of the amount in the pool. A player winning no trick is looed—that is, he must contribute to the pool, as may be agreed, either the original stake or the amount already in the pool (subject to a limit agreed on beforehand). If each player takes a trick, so that no one is looed, each contributes the same stake as at first to form a new pool.

Each player has the option of "passing"—that is, throwing in his hand altogether—in which case he cannot be looed. Anyone taking miss is bound to play. If all pass except the dealer, he is entitled to the pool. If all except one have passed, the dealer *must* play, with the option of taking miss if it is still available, but he may do so either on his own account or "for the pool." In the latter case, he cannot be looed, but the value of any tricks he may make remains in the pool to await the result of the next round. He may look at his hand before declaring what he proposes to do, but if he takes and looks at miss without previously announcing his decision, he is bound to play on his own account.

The Bergen Game (2 players):   Each player draws six cards. The player holding the lowest double (in this game known as a double-header) leads, and scores two. If neither player holds a double, they each alternately draw another card until a double-header appears. This is then played and scores two. The second player must follow suit or, if he cannot, must draw another card.

If this does not enable him to follow suit, he says, "Go," and the leader in turn plays or draws from the pool. Whenever a player succeeds in making both ends of the line alike—say, two fives, or two sixes—this is also counted as a double-header, and the player scores two. Doubles (except the first one played) have no scoring value in themselves, but if one of the ends of the line is a double, and the next player's card makes the other end of the same value, or if a double is played at either end of an existing double-header, it is known as a triple-header, and counts three points.

Fifteen points constitutes game, the player making domino—that is, the first to exhaust his hand—scores one. If the game ends because both players are blocked, the player holding the smallest number of pips, and no double, is the winner of that hand and scores one. If, however, the holder of the smallest hand holds a double and his opponent does not, the latter is the winner. If both hold doubles, the player with the smallest number of doubles, irrespective of denomination, wins. If each has a double, the holder of the smaller one wins. When a player is within two points of game, a double-header will not give him game but will only count as one. Similarly, when a player is within three of winning, a triple-header counts only as two.

SOLITAIRE

This ancient game (similar to Chinese checkers and not to be confused with the card game solitaire), once a feature in every parlor, is now enjoying a comeback. Sets of solitaire, consisting of a board and thirty-three marbles, can be bought at any good toy shop. The board is marked with 33 holes arranged as follows on page 93.

With all the marbles except one placed on the board, the object of the game is to clear the board of every marble but one, leaving this last in the space first made vacant. The marbles are removed by being passed over by an adjacent marble very much as in checkers, except that the marbles move vertically or horizontally in either direction. They

cannot move diagonally. Thus if spaces number 3 and 9 are
vacant, the marble at number 1 may remove marble 2 by
jumping over it to space 3 or, alternatively, it may remove
marble 4 by jumping to space 9.

The player should pose his own problems and then try
to solve them, but the keys to three problems are given here
to demonstrate the general principles and systems of play
that can be applied to the game. For the sake of brevity, the
moves only are given. It should always be remembered that a
marble passed over by another is removed from the board and
that no piece can move unless it *does* so take another piece.

Problem No. 1 (This is the most usually played game and is
known as the Center Hole game.)

Remove the center marble, No. 17

    1:   5 to 17
    2: 12 to 10
    3:   3 to 11
    4: 18 to   6
    5:   1 to   3, and again, on to 11
    6: 30 to 18
    7: 27 to 25
    8: 24 to 26
    9: 13 to 27, and again, on to 25

10: 22 to 24
11: 31 to 23
12: 16 to 28
13: 33 to 31, and again, to 23
14: 4 to 16
15: 7 to 9
16: 10 to 8
17: 21 to 7, and again, to 9
18: 24 to 10, and again, to 8, 22, 24 and 26
19: 19 to 17
20: 16 to 18
21: 11 to 25
22: 26 to 24
23: 29 to 17, which was the starting point.

Problem No. 2   The above problem may be adapted to clear
the board starting with ball 2, ball 20, or ball 32.

Remove the ball at 14
 1: 16 to 14
 2: 4 to 16
 3: 17 to 15
 4: 6 to 4
 5: 29 to 17, and again, on to 5
 6: 2 to 10
 7: 18 to 6
 8: 3 to 11
 9: 20 to 18, and again, on to 6
10: 13 to 11
11: 6 to 18
12: 26 to 24
13: 33 to 25
14: 24 to 26
15: 27 to 25
16: 31 to 33
17: 18 to 30
18: 33 to 25
19: 22 to 24
20: 25 to 23
21: 7 to 9
22: 10 to 8
23: 1 to 9
24: 28 to 16, and again, on to 4
25: 21 to 7, and again, on to 9
26: 4 to 16, and again, on to 14, the starting point.

Problem No. 3 This problem can be adapted when using any of the corner balls as starters.

Remove the ball at 1
```
 1:  9 to  1
 2:  7 to  9
 3: 10 to  8
 4: 21 to  7
 5:  7 to  9
 6: 22 to  8
 7:  8 to 10
 8:  6 to  4
 9:  1 to  9
10: 18 to  6
11:  3 to 11
12: 20 to 18
13: 18 to  6
14: 30 to 18
15: 27 to 25
16: 24 to 26
17: 28 to 30
18: 33 to 25
19: 18 to 30
20: 31 to 33
21: 33 to 25
22: 26 to 24
23: 16 to 18
24: 23 to 25
25: 25 to 11
26:  6 to 18
27: 13 to 11
28: 18 to  6
29:  9 to 11
30: 11 to  3
31:  3 to  1, the starting point.
```

If the above problems are studied, it will be seen that it is possible to start and end a game on any point of the board selected. When the game is thoroughly mastered, any desired combination can be played for.

DIXON PUBLIC
LIBRARY
DIXON, ILLINOIS

4

Card Games

he history of playing cards has long been of interest to scholars, and yet it is still not known where and when they originated. We do know, however, that for nearly six hundred years, good round card games have provided excellent family entertainment in Europe and that it will take something far more powerful than radio and television to make card playing a thing of the past.

As a social pastime, card playing (along with other indoor recreations in general) reached its peak in the nineteenth century. Faced with the isolation of living in crowded towns, with every evening free and with the newly invented gaslight discouraging early retirement, people found card playing an absorbing pastime for the evenings—especially in the winter months.

There is a close connection between the introduction of gaslighting and the increase in popularity of card playing. In 1813, the foundation was laid for the London and Westminster Gas Company, which built three manufacturing stations in London and laid fifteen miles of mains. By 1861, so many gas companies had sprung up in the metropolis and other large towns in Great Britian that they were officially recorded as "innumerable." During that same period, "innumerable" card games had been invented or devised, some being completely original, others based on older games. They include Écarté, Newmarket, Euchre, Poker, Bézique, Bridge, and all the derivations and varieties of the latter game. In addition, many of the older games, such as Matrimony, Brag, Cassino, Faro, Speculation, and Pope Joan were revived.

Compiling this section has been a matter of careful selection, to include those games which will still have appeal. This selection ranges from the simplest children's games to some that will appeal to the most sophisticated card player.

The game of Whist, together with all its variations and relations, has not been included, for it is a subject that requires a book to itself. Also excluded are the other "serious" games, such as Poker and Cribbage and "professional" gambling games like Baccarat, although all these were in vogue during the Victorian era. However, some of the games described are based on Whist, and, for those who have no knowledge of this game, the basic principles are explained under German Whist (p. 104).

CARD GAMES FOR FUN

Snap (2-6 players):   This ever-popular card game is ideal for a mixture of ages, although often a cause of bitterness for the older players, who tend to lose repeatedly. From two to six players may take part, two packs of cards being used if the number of players is four or more.

All the cards are shuffled and dealt face down to each player. The hands are taken up but are kept face down, and the players must not look at them. Starting from the dealer's left, each player in turn takes the top card from his hand and lays it face up in front of him. This play continues until two of the exposed cards coincide—that is, two kings, two tens, two twos, etc. When this happens, the owners of the two cards have the opportunity (presuming, that is, that they have noticed the phenomenon) of calling "Snap!" The first of the two to do so takes up all the cards played by both.

It should be noted that the other players do not have the right of calling but must wait until one of their cards coincides with another. The game continues until eventually one player holds all the cards. If a player is left with only one card, this remains on the table until it coincides with another, when its holder must call "Snap" first or lose his card and drop out of the game altogether.

Animal Grab (3-6 players):   This is another form of Snap. Each player is given the distinctive cry of some animal—dog, cat, sheep, cow, etc.—and the game is then played in the usual way, except that when two players turn up similar cards, instead of crying "Snap," they give the cry belonging to the *other* person. The tendency is for the players to give their own sound, or to search their memories for the noise belonging to the other person. The one who gives the right cry first wins the cards.

Grimace Snap (3-6 players):   In this game the rules of ordinary Snap are followed except that when two similar cards come up, the players do not cry "Snap" but each endeavors to make the other laugh—to which end they may do anything but speak or touch each other. The first one to laugh loses his cards.

Grab Cork or *Silent Snap* (3-6 players):   This is played like ordinary Snap except that when two cards are alike, instead of shouting "Snap," the players must try to secure a cork that is in the middle of the table. This is a most suitable game for the younger members of the family.

Old Maid: This simple card game is suitable for two or more players. A special Old Maid pack may be purchased, or you may use an ordinary deck minus one of the queens—any one may be removed. The cards are then shuffled and dealt to all the players until the pack is exhausted. Each player then looks at his hand and discards any pairs that it may contain. When all the pairs have been thrown out, the player on the left of the dealer offers his hand, face down, to the player on his lefthand side, who draws any one card of his choice. If this card should pair with one already in his hand, he discards that pair; if not, it remains in his hand with the rest of his cards. Either way, he then offers his hand to the player on his left.

In the course of the game all the cards will be paired and thrown out. It is the object of the game to try to pass the odd queen to the next player, for the holder of it at the end of the game is the Old Maid.

This game can be varied by discarding not necessarily a queen but any *unknown* card. The game gains an extra interest in this form, for no one has any idea which card in the pack will make him or her the Old Maid.

Beggar-My-Neighbor or *Strip Jack Naked:* This game is suitable for two or more players. The pack is shuffled, and one player deals out the entire pack equally. The player on the left of the dealer leads, and the players each turn up a card in turn. When certain cards are turned up by a player, his neighbor on the left must pay him a certain number of cards as forfeit: 1 card is paid for a jack, 2 for a queen, 3 for a king, and 4 for an ace.

When payment has been made, the player being paid picks up all the cards that have been laid down and puts them underneath those in his hand. If, while paying a forfeit, a player himself turns up an ace, king, queen or jack, he stops paying and is paid in turn by *his* left-hand neighbor. The game continues until all the cards are in the hand of one player—he is the winner. Any player who loses all his cards is out of the game.

Donkey (six to thirteen players): This game is particularly suitable for children's parties when a little light relief is required. Ideally it is played by thirteen players, allowing the full pack to be distributed, four to a player. If there are only twelve players, then all the twos are removed from the pack; for eleven players, twos and threes are removed, etc. The cards are then dealt, four to each player, and are held in the hand ready for play. On the word "go" from the dealer, all the players *simultaneously* take a card from their hands and pass it face down to the player on their left.

This continues at speed, each player retaining the cards he requires to make up four of a kind and passing on those cards which he does not want. The moment one of the players obtains his four of a kind, he lays them face up on the table, sits back, and folds his arms. As soon as another player notices this, he does the same. The last player to sit back is the loser of that round, and he is given the letter D, the first letter of Donkey. If he should lose a second time, he becomes DO, and the game continues until one player has lost six times, which, of course, makes him the DONKEY.

Fish or *Pelmanism:*   This is a memory game, suitable for any number of cards. With large numbers, two packs of cards may be used. The cards are shuffled and then laid out in rows face down on the table. The first player turns up any two cards. If they make a pair, he takes them up and puts them face down in front of him. This entitles him to another turn, and he turns up two more cards. If they are not a pair, he turns them face down again, and the turn passes to the player on his left.

After the first few rounds, the positions of certain cards will become known to the players, and those who remember them will collect the most pairs. When all the cards have been paired, the player with the most is the winner.

The Seven Blows of Circumstance (four or more players): This is an exciting game and very suitable for parties, for it will be enjoyed by all from the age of seven upward. The ace, two, three, four, five, six, and seven of Hearts are taken from the pack and put on the table face up and in numerical order to form a circle. These are the Seven Blows of Circumstance, and the center of the ring is the pool.

One card is then dealt to each player from the remainder of the pack and with it a small piece of paper bearing the player's name. The object of the game is to get possession of as low a card as possible (ace counting low) for the player with the highest card has to put on a "blow"—that is, he must put his name paper on the ace of Hearts and, as the game proceeds, every time his card is the highest, he must move his name one up, until, after the seven of Hearts is reached, he is "submerged" in the pool. There he stays until the end of the game or until some other player speaks to him.

A player in the pool may use any reasonable device to get another player to make the mistake of speaking to him, and if he is successful, he is taken out of the pool and can begin his "life" afresh. The player who spoke to him is automatically raised to the seventh Blow of Circumstance.

After the cards have been dealt, one to each player, the game proceeds as follows. The first player to have been dealt a card has the option of passing it (if he considers it too high) to his left-hand neighbor and receiving his in exchange. The first player must not look at his card (under penalty of adding a blow to his account) until all the other players have changed (or refused to change) their cards. The second player looks at the card dealt to him, or to the one received in exchange for it, and if he thinks it too high, he can pass it on in turn to Number 3. This goes on until all but the dealer have passed or exchanged. The dealer may exchange his card for a random one in the pack if he wishes.

Then all the cards are turned up (all the players who have exchanged seeing their cards for the first time), and the player with the highest card has to take a Blow of Circumstance. Each player takes his turn as dealer, and the game goes on until all the players but one are drowned in the pool, the survivor being the winner.

Ranter-Go-Round (4 or more players): This is a more serious version of the previous game. Any number of players can join in, but each must be supplied with three counters, or lives—the object of the game being to see which player will succeed in keeping at least one of his lives, high cards being desirable.

A full pack of cards is shuffled, and one card is dealt face down to each player. The players look at their cards, and the one on the left of the dealer, if he thinks his card is too low, has the option of exchanging it with his left-hand neighbor. The neighbor must make the exchange if asked. He can then change cards with *his* left-hand neighbor, and so on around the table until the dealer is reached, and, as he has no one with whom to exchange, he is allowed to take the top card from the remainder of the pack.

The players one by one turn up their cards, starting with the player on the dealer's left and the possessor of the lowest card (aces counting low) loses a life. If two players have cards of the same value and these cards are the lowest, the player who last turned up his card loses a life. The deal moves on to the next player.

If a player has given to his right-hand neighbor a card that is lower than the one received in the exchange, he will of course *stand* on that card—that is, he will not offer it in exchange to the player on *his* left, for he will be well aware that at least *one* card lower than his is out. No player may exchange more than once.

The vicissitudes of fortune in Ranter-Go-Round are remarkable. For instance, a player may keep all his three lives until only he and one other are left in the game, and then he may lose them all in three successive rounds. On the other hand, a player may lose two lives very early on in the game and yet carry on with the remaining one to win.

Thank You: This is a game for four players and requires a good memory. The whole pack is dealt, and the object is for each player to get as many sets of four as possible. The player to the left of the dealer asks any person he chooses for a certain card. He must not, however, ask for a card unless he holds at least one of the same value in his own hand.

For example, A, with a five of Clubs in his hand, may ask C for the five of Hearts. If C has that card, he must give it up to A, and A may then proceed to ask him or any other player for another card, and so on. If, however, a player is asked for a card he does not possess, the right of asking passes to him.

In addition, if a player takes a card from another player, he must say, "Thank you," *before* he touches it; otherwise he loses to the other player both the card and the right of asking for another. In the case of A asking C for the five of Hearts and not saying, "Thank you," C will know that A possesses at least one five and has, therefore, a good chance of obtaining it.

At first it is entirely a matter of chance whether the right person is asked, but as the game progresses, both memory and deduction play their parts. For instance, A has the seven of Hearts and the seven of Diamonds and B asks C for the seven of Spades and is refused it. A then knows and must remember that B must have the seven of Clubs and that D must have the seven of Spades.

As soon as a player completes a set of four, he lays it face down on the table in front of him. When all the cards are thus laid down, the players aim at getting possession of the complete pack by asking each other for sets. This part of the game is played in the same way as the first part, the player who completed the last set being the first to ask. The same rule of saying "Thank you" applies. The omission of these words may cost a player the game, for the player who passed the last set, if not thanked for it, may retaliate by demanding all the sets his opponent has collected.

The Book of Fate (4-8 players):   This is a unique card game, for it involves not only forfeits but the possible exchange of numerous kisses. The president of the game takes a pack of cards and deals three to each player. He keeps the remainder himself; these he may consult when necessary, although he has nothing to do with the game beyond superintending it. Each player conceals his cards from his neighbors.

After dealing, the president asks the player on his left: "Have you read the Book of Fate?" The player replies, "Yes, I have read the Book of Fate." The president then asks, "What did you read in the Book of Fate?" and the player replies, "I read *so and so* [naming any card, provided it is not in his own hand])."

The president then consults the reserve pack, and if the named card is found there, the player naming it pays a forfeit. If not, the others examine their hands, and the one in whose hand it is found gives it up to the president. At this point the person naming the card and the one in whose hand it is found must, if they are of different sexes, exchange a kiss; otherwise both pay forfeits.

The game now proceeds thus. The person previously questioned now becomes the questioner and asks the player on his left, "Have you read the Book of Fate?"—and so on until all the cards have returned to the hands of the president.

Should anyone in the course of the game ask for a card that has already been dealt with, he must pay a forfeit. Consequently, to avoid disputes, the president should take care to keep apart from the rest of the pack the cards already asked for and to conceal them from the players so as to give no hint of what has gone before.

It must be thoroughly understood that any card found in the hand of the player who asks for it is evidence of immense stupidity and a severe forfeit should be imposed. In the case of a gentleman, I'm in a Well (page 138) would be appropriate; in that of a lady, she should be compelled either to Run the Gauntlet (page 137) or Perform the Parrot (page 131).

Cheat (3 or more players):   A full pack of 52 cards is dealt equally to the players. Any cards remaining are placed face down in the center of the table. When all the players have examined their cards, the player on the dealer's left leads any card face down on the table, naming its denomination. Thus, if his card is a five, he must say, "Five." The next player must now play a six on top of the five, again face down, and call, "Six." It is not necessary, however, for the card laid down to be the same as the number called.

The play goes on, seven follows six, eight follows seven, and so on. After a king, the next card declared is "Ace." Any one of the company is at liberty to challenge a player to show the last card played by calling out, "Cheat." In this case, the player must show his card, and if it is not what he claimed it to be, he must pick up all the cards previously laid down on the table. If he proves himself honest, then his detractor must pick up the cards.

After a challenge, the player to the left of the one challenged plays any card he likes to the table. It is legitimate to cheat also by playing two cards at once. The player who first gets rid of all his cards is the winner.

Truth (4–8 players): Two packs of cards are required for this game, one of which is placed face down in front of the dealer, and the other dealt to the company, including the dealer, card by card, until it is exhausted. The dealer then asks a question concerning the company, at the same time turning up a card from the undealt pack. Whatever card this is, the dealer calls for its counterpart from the players and the holder of it must reply to the question.

Ridiculous personal questions create the most fun. Turning up the queen of Hearts, for instance, the dealer may ask, "Who is it that thinks he is the most good-looking person here?" The holder of the corresponding card must then stand up and admit his vanity. As a compensation for this, however, he (or she) is entitled to put the next question. As the question-and-answer cards are produced, they are laid aside, and the game proceeds until both packs are finished.

CARD GAMES FOR MONEY

German Whist (two players):   This is the simplest game of Whist and it incorporates all the basic principles of Whist proper. The game is for two players only. The cards rank as follows (ace high): ace, king, queen, jack, ten, nine, eight, seven, six, five, four, three, two. The four suits are equal in value, but the suit that is turned up as *trumps* has precedence over the other suits. When playing for tricks, each player *must* (providing he is able) follow suit. If he cannot follow suit, the player may, if the card led is not a trump, play a trump (in which case he wins the trick). Or he may "throw away"—that is, play a card that is not a trump—and lose the trick irrespective of the value of the card he plays.

The players cut for deal, the highest card winning, and the dealer gives, one by one, thirteen cards to his opponent and to himself. The remainder of the pack, known as the stock, is then laid face down on the table, and the top card is turned up to determine the trump suit. This "turn-up" card is now played for as follows.

The nondealer selects any card from his hand and lays it face up on the table. The dealer now plays to that card according to the rules above, following suit if he can. Whoever plays the highest card takes the trick and the turn-up card. The trick he lays face down on the table beside him, the turn-up card he adds to his hand. The loser of the trick takes the next card from the stock and adds it to *his* hand. The next card on the stock is turned up and played for in the same way. (Remember that the first turn-up determines trumps for the whole hand.) The winner of a trick takes the lead for the next.

When the twenty-six cards in the stock are exhausted, the play for tricks continues until no cards remain in the players' hands. The tricks are then counted, and the player with the greater number scores the difference between his tricks and his opponent's (that is, if a player makes 16 tricks and his opponent 10, he scores 6 points). A score limit, say 50 points, should be set.

Bézique: This is a game for two players, and when it was first introduced to England in 1861, it enjoyed great popularity. The game is played with two Piquet packs (that is, two packs from which the twos, threes, fours, fives, and sixes have been removed). The two packs are shuffled together. (If four play, four packs must be used.)

After shuffling and cutting, the dealer gives eight cards (by dealing three, two, and three) to each player. The remainder of the pack—the talon—is left on the table and the top card is turned up to one side for trumps. If this turn-up card is a seven, the dealer scores 10.

The game now begins, the play of each hand being in two parts: first, each player plays a card from his hand, taking in exchange a card from the pack until this is exhausted; second, the eight cards that remain to each player are played out under different scoring conditions.

The preliminary play is as follows: The nondealer leads to the first trick, to which the dealer will then play a card. The winner of the trick takes the top card from the talon (this is not the turned-up trump card), his opponent takes the next card. Play continues until this pile is exhausted. After the first turned-up card, the cards on the talon are left face down.

The value of the cards in making the tricks is as follows: ace, ten, king, queen, jack, nine, eight, seven. In this preliminary part of the play, there is no need to follow suit. The only objects of taking tricks at this stage of the game are (a) to cash in on aces and tens (any ace or ten included in a trick scores 10 for the winner of it) and (b) to make a Declaration. A Declaration can only be made by a player immediately after taking a trick. It consists in laying the appropriate cards face up on the table and mentioning the scoring combination claimed. A card that has been declared stays on the table until it is played. The exposed cards are led or played to a trick on the table in exactly the same way as cards in the hand. A Declaration is scored as it is claimed. They are as follows:

> Common Marriage (king and queen of any suit other than trumps) 20 points
> Royal Marriage (king and queen of the trump suit) 40 points
> Bézique (queen of Spades and knave of Diamonds) 40 points
> Four jacks 40 points
> Four queens 60 points
> Four kings 80 points
> Four aces 100 points
> Sequence (ace, ten, king, queen, jack of the trump suit) 250 points
> Double Bézique (both queens of Spades and both jacks of Diamonds) 500 points

As mentioned above, any ace or ten included in tricks scores 10 points for the winner of the trick.

Finally, a player holding the seven of trumps in his hand

may, immediately after taking a trick, exchange it for the turned-up trump card. Exchanging the seven ranks as a Declaration, and another Declaration cannot be made at the same time.

Only one Declaration can be made at a time. Thus a player cannot put down a trump Sequence and score both for the Sequence and for a Royal Marriage.

The first stage of the game goes on until there are only two cards left that are not in the possession of the players—that is, the bottom card of the pack and the card turned up to indicate the trump suit (or the seven that has been exchanged for it). The winner of the last trick takes the bottom card, and the loser takes the turned-up card.

The second part of the play is sometimes called the Play-Off. Each player takes into his hand any exposed cards he has on the table, and the eight tricks are played out. At this stage, a player must follow suit; if he cannot do this, he may trump or discard. No Declarations can be made but players continue to score 10 points for aces or tens won in tricks. The scores are added up, and game is usually taken to be 1,000 points.

Euchre

This game is still very popular in the United States, and can be played by two, three, or four players. It is played with a Piquet pack of thirty-two cards—that is, with all cards below seven (ace counting high) removed. The cards rank as in Whist, except that the jack of trumps, known as the Right Bower, and the jack of the suit of the same color, the Left Bower, take temporary precedence over all other cards.

Thus, when Hearts are trumps, the cards rank as follows: jack of Hearts, jack of Diamonds, ace, king, queen, ten, nine, eight and seven of Hearts. The Left Bower is considered for the time being to belong to the trump suit, so that if this card is led, the trump suit is played to it. A still higher trump is sometimes, by agreement, introduced. This is the joker, known in Euchre as Best Bower, and it takes precedence even over the Right Bower. If the joker chances to be the turned-up card, the card next in order decides the trump suit.

Two-Handed Euchre: The players having cut for deal, five

cards are dealt (by twos and then threes, or vice versa) to each player. The eleventh card is turned up by way of trump. If the nondealer thinks his hand good enough, with the suit of the turned-up card as trumps, to make three tricks, he says, referring to that card, "I order it up." This fixes that suit as trumps. The dealer discards the worst card of his own hand, placing it face down under the pack, and the turned-up card is then considered to form part of his hand. He does not, however, actually take it into his hand until the first trick has been played. If the nondealer does not consider his hand good for three tricks, or is of the opinion that he would be likely to gain by a change of the trump suit, he says, "I pass," and the dealer examines his own cards from the same point of view. If he thinks his hand is good enough with the existing trump suit to make three tricks, he says, "I take it up," and proceeds to place, as before, one card under the pack. If he does not think his hand safe for three, he says, "I turn it down," and places the turned-up card below the rest of the pack.

This annuls the trump suit, and the nondealer now has the option of saying what suit will be trumps. He considers what will best suit his hand, and says, "Make it Hearts [or whichever suit is best]," accordingly. If he decides to make it *of the same color* as the previous turned-up card (Spades in place of Clubs, or Hearts in place of Diamonds), he is said to "make it next," if otherwise, to "cross the suit." If, even with the privilege of making the trump what he pleases, he doubts his ability to win three tricks, he again passes, and the dealer makes it what best suits him. If he too has such a bad hand that he thinks it safer to pass again, the cards are thrown up, and the deal passes.

The trump suit having been made by the one or the other player, the nondealer leads a card, and the dealer plays to it. The second player must follow suit if he can, subject to the qualification that (as already stated) if the Left Bower is led, a trump must be played to it. The higher card wins, and the winner of the trick leads to the next.

The player who has ordered up, taken up (except in obedience to order), or made the trump, has thereby tacitly undertaken to win at least three tricks. If he makes less than this number, he is "euchred," and his opponent scores two. If he makes three tricks, he wins the point, and scores one. Four tricks are no better than three, but if he makes all five, he wins a "march," which scores two. The nonchallenging player is not under any obligation to win, but scores if his adversary fails to do so. A score of five points constitutes Game.

Four-Handed Euchre: Where four players take part, two play in partnership against the other two, partners facing each other. Five cards are dealt to each, and the twenty-first is turned up by way of trump. The elder hand (to the left of the dealer) declares whether he will order up the trump card or pass. If he passes, the option goes to the dealer's partner; but he expresses his position differently, since he is playing with a partner. If he thinks his hand good for two or more tricks, he says, "I assist." This is considered a call to his partner (the dealer) to take up the trump, which he does accordingly, having no choice in the matter. If the second player passes, the option rests with the third player, who orders it up or passes, as his hand may warrant.

In the latter case, the dealer decides for himself whether to take it up or to turn it down. If the trump has either been ordered up or taken up voluntarily by the dealer, the play proceeds as in the two-handed game. If, on the other hand, the dealer turns it down, the players, beginning with the elder hand, are invited in succession to make it what they please; the challenging party in either case being bound, in conjunction with his partner, to make three tricks, under penalty of being euchred.

A player with an unusually strong hand may elect to go alone. In such a case, his partner turns his cards face down on the table, and leaves the lone hand, as he is termed, to play the game singly against the two opponents. If a player going alone manages to win all five tricks, he scores *four* (instead of two for the march); but if he makes three or four tricks only, he scores one for the point in the ordinary manner.

Three-Handed Euchre: In this form of the game each plays for his own hand. The value of the march and point are the same as in the two-handed game, but if the challenging player is euchred, each of his adversaries scores two points. If this should carry them both out, the elder hand is the winner. To avoid this, which is hardly a satisfactory termination for the younger hand, another method of scoring is sometimes adopted, the points for the euchre being *deducted* from the score of the euchred player, who is set back accordingly. Should he have made no points toward game, he is considered to owe the points for the euchre; so that a player, standing at love when euchred, has seven points to make before he can win.

Making the Score: Methods of scoring at Euchre are unusual. The score is usually kept by means of spare playing cards, a three and a four (of any suit) being used by each side. The three face upward, with the four turned down upon it, indicates one (however many pips may chance to be exposed). The four face upward, with the three turned down upon it, indicates two. The face of the three being uppermost counts three; and the face of the four being uppermost counts four.

Another method of keeping the score is by means of a cross chalked at the outset of the game on the table beside each player. One is scored by rubbing out the center of the cross, leaving the four arms still standing, and these in turn are rubbed out, one for each point which the player becomes entitled to score.

Loo

Loo was already well established in the seventeenth century and during the nineteenth it enjoyed greater popularity than perhaps any other round game. Toward the end of the century, however, it began to be superseded by Napoleon, Whist, and Poker. There is no limit to the number of players, but six or seven make the best game. There are many versions of the game but only the two leading varieties, known as Three-Card and Five-Card Loo, are dealt with here.

Three-Card Loo: The full pack is used, the cards ranking as in Whist (ace, king, queen, jack, ten, nine, etc.). The dealer places an agreed number of his counters (either three or some multiple of three) in the pool. Sometimes each player contributes an agreed amount to start the pool, but this is a matter of arrangement. Three cards are then dealt, one by one, to each player, with an extra hand, known as "miss." The card next following is then turned up and fixes the trump suit. The dealer then asks each player in succession, beginning with the elder hand, whether he will play or "take miss."

If he holds a good hand, he will elect to play it;

otherwise he has the option of either taking miss—that is, taking the extra hand in place of his own—or of passing— that is, throwing up his hand altogether for that round. If miss is declined, the same offer is made to the next player, but as soon as miss is taken, the remaining players have only two alternatives: either to play the hand they hold, or to pass. A player who has taken miss is bound to play. The cards he has discarded, together with those of any players who pass, are thrown face downward in the middle of the table, and no player may look at them.

Should one player take miss and all the rest throw in their cards, he is entitled to the pool. Should only one player declare to play, and he has not taken miss, the dealer may either play his own cards or take miss on his own account, but if he does not care to do either, he is bound to take miss and to play on behalf of the pool—that is, the proceeds of any tricks he may make must remain in the pool to await the result of the next round. In the event that everyone except the dealer passes, the dealer is entitled to the pool.

The elder hand of those who have declared to play now leads a card, but he is subject to certain rules. If he has two trumps, he must lead one of them. If he holds the ace of trumps, he is bound to lead it, or if an ace is turned up, and he holds the king of the same suit, he is bound to lead the latter. If only two persons have declared to play, and the elder player holds two or more trumps, he must lead the *highest,* unless his highest trumps are in sequence or of equal value (for instance, where a player holds the seven and nine of trumps, the eight having been turned up, the seven and nine are then of equal value) and he may lead either of them. With more than three declared players, the last-mentioned rule does not apply.

The other players play in rotation to the card led, subject to these rules. Each player must follow suit, if possible, and he must "head the trick"—that is, he must play a higher card to it, if he is able to do so. If unable to follow suit, he is bound to trump, or if the trick is already trumped, he must overtrump if he possibly can. The winner of each trick leads to the next. He is under the same obligations as the original leader and is further bound to lead a trump, if he has one.

When the hand has been played out, the pool is divided, in the proportion of one third to each trick. Suppose, for instance, that five players have played, that one of them has taken two tricks and another has taken one trick. The first takes two thirds and the second one third of the pool. The remaining three players are "looed"—that is, they must each pay to the pool the same amount that was originally placed there. These loos, with a like contribution from the new dealer, form the pool for the next hand.

It may happen that only three players declare to play, and that each of them takes one trick. In such a case, no one is looed, and the only fund to form the pool for the next round is the contribution of the dealer (plus the agreed contribution, if any, of the other players). The next hand in such a case is known as a single, and it is usual in such a case to make a "force" or a "must," meaning that everyone, whatever his cards, is bound to play. This necessarily produces some loos and consequently a pool for the next hand. In the case of a must, there is no miss.

In circles in which the gambling interest of Loo is the main one, the payment for a loo is sometimes made equal to the amount that may chance to be in the pool at that particular time. This form of Loo is known as Unlimited Loo, for the amount of a loo tends consequently to increase, until the occurrence of a single—that is, three players only declaring to play and each taking one trick—brings it back to its normal proportions. In Unlimited Loo, the sums mount rapidly, and the game should be avoided by prudent players unless a reasonable maximum is fixed, beyond which no advance is permitted.

Five-Card Loo: In this game five cards are dealt to each player, the card next following being turned up for the trump suit. There are, therefore, five tricks to be played for, and contributions to the pool are made divisible by five accordingly. In the five-card version, there is no miss but each player, beginning with the elder hand, is entitled to discard as many cards as he pleases, the dealer replacing them with a like number from the stock. Each player has the option either to play or pass, but once having drawn new cards, he is bound to play.

In this version of the game the jack of Clubs, known as Pam, is made into a sort of paramount trump and takes precedence even over the ace of trumps. The rules as to leading, following suit, and "heading the trick" are the same as in the three-card game. If, however, the ace of trumps is led, and the holder says, as he plays it, "Pam, be civil," then the holder of Pam is bound to pass the trick and not play Pam unless he cannot follow suit.

Special value in this game is given to a flush—that is, five cards of the same suit or four cards of the same suit and Pam. The holder of such a hand at once turns up his hand and "loos the board"—that is, he wins every trick as of right, without playing his hand. No one, in this case, is allowed to throw in his hand, and all except the holder of the flush are looed. A flush of trumps has priority over one in a plain suit; in the case of two flushes in trumps, or two in plain suits, the better cards win. The holder of the losing flush, or of Pam, if in the hand of one of the losers, is exempt from payment. In all other respects the game is the same as Three-Card Loo.

All Fours

Known in America as Old Sledge or Seven Up, this game is usually played by two or four players with a full pack of cards which rank in play as in Whist. The game is played for seven points.

There are four different items which count toward the score, whence the name All Fours. These items are as follows:

High. The highest trump out, scoring one to its original holder.
Low. The lowest trump out, scoring one to its original owner.
Jack. The jack of trumps, scoring one to the dealer, if turned up; otherwise one to the winner of the trick in which it falls.
Game. Scoring one to the holder of the more valuable cards (trumps or otherwise) in the tricks won by him, according to the following scale.

For each ten   10
For each ace   4
For each king   3
For each queen   2
For each jack   1

If both of the players score the point for game, or if neither party holds any card that counts toward game, the elder hand scores the point.

Two-Handed All Fours: The players cut for deal. The dealer gives six cards to each, turning up the thirteenth card as trump. If the owner of the elder hand is dissatisfied with his cards, he may say, "I beg." In that case the dealer is bound either to allow him (by the phrase "take one") to score one point, or to give each player three more cards from the pack, turning up the following one by way of a fresh trump card. If this should be of the same suit as the original trump, the dealer is bound to give three more cards to each, again turning up the seventh, until a new suit does actually turn up.

If the turned-up card is a jack, the dealer scores one, this taking precedence over any other score. If, by reason of the elder hand begging, there is a further deal, and the dealer a second time turns up a jack, he again scores one. The elder hand leads any card he pleases. His opponent may choose to follow suit *or* trump. If he cannot do either, he throws away. If he has a card of the suit led and neither follows suit nor trumps,. he becomes liable to the penalty of the revoke, as will be explained.

In scoring, the order of precedence is High, Low, Jack, Game, as shown above, subject to the contingency of jack's having been the turned-up card, the point for this being scored before the hand is played.

The play is mainly directed toward capturing the jack, and such cards as may score toward Game.

Some players score a point whenever the opponent does not follow suit or trump. Some, again, make it the rule that each player must count his score without looking at his tricks under penalty of losing one or more points, as may be agreed, in the event of a miscalculation. It should be arranged beforehand which rules are to be followed.

Four-Handed All Fours: The players cut to decide who shall be partners—the two highest playing against the two lowest and facing each other as at Whist. The right to the first deal is decided by the cut, the highest dealing. Afterward the players deal in turn.

The dealer and the elder hand alone look at their cards in the first instance, the option of begging resting with the latter. The other two players must not take up their cards till the dealer has decided whether he will "give one" or "run the cards" for a new trump. The players play in succession as in

Whist. In other respects the play is the same as in the two-handed game.

Brag

Brag (4–8 players): Brag is the parent of Poker and is one of the oldest English card games. There are two versions, Single Brag and Three Stake Brag. Both are played with a full pack of cards. The ace of Diamonds, jack of Clubs, and nine of Diamonds, known as braggers, are in effect jokers—that is, they are allowed to stand for any other card at the pleasure of the holder. The other cards rank as in Whist (ace, king, queen, jack, ten, nine, etc.).

Single Stake Brag: The dealer starts by putting up any stake up to the agreed limit and then deals three cards, singly, to each player. Each player in turn looks at his cards and either "brags"—puts up a stake equal to that of the dealer—or passes—drops out of the game. Any player may raise the dealer's stake and, in any case, each player who stays in the game must put up as much as the highest stake or abandon his hand, thus losing any stake he may have placed up to then.

If no one is willing to brag, the dealer receives a single counter from each of the other players remaining in the game, and the deal passes to the left for the next round. Should any player brag a stake that no other player is willing to meet, then he takes the pool without having to show his hand. Any player who is "called" or "seen" by another must show his hand, and the best hand takes the pool—the order of value of the hands being as follows:

1. Three aces *natural* (one that contains no bragger, although the ace of Diamonds here ranks as a natural ace).

2. Three aces, including one or two braggers.

3. Three kings or other smaller cards in due order, the higher being preferred to the lower and, between those of equal value, natural threes being preferred to those made with the aid of braggers.

4. Pairs from ace downward, with the same preference for naturals.

5. In default of any pair, the hand holding the best

single card, the ace of Diamonds ranking highest, after it any other ace, and so on.

Between the holders of absolutely equal cards, the elder hand has preference.

Three Stake Brag: Three separate stakes are made at the outset by each player, the winning of each being determined in a different manner. Three cards are dealt to each player, but the last card of each is dealt face up. The best card so dealt entitles its holder to the first stake. The second stake becomes the property of the holder of the best brag hand, the game being fought out as in Single Brag. The third stake goes to the player whose cards when totaled are nearest thirty-one; aces count as eleven, and all court cards count ten. Any player whose cards fall short of that number may, if he wishes and in due turn, draw a card or cards from the pack in the hope of amending his point. If he overdraws, he is out of the game.

Other Games for Money

Lansquenet: This is a game of considerable antiquity. It was popular in the Middle Ages with the German mercenaries known as *lansquenets.* It is essentially a gambling game of pure chance.

Any number of persons may play. A full pack of fifty-two cards is usually used, but sometimes two packs are called for, shuffled together.

After the shuffle, the dealer lays two cards face up by his left hand—these are known as hand cards. He then deals a card for himself and a fourth card, known as the *réjouissance* ("rejoicing") card, in the center of the table. It is on this last card that the rest of the players bet. If either the dealer's card or the *réjouissance* card is of the same denomination as either of the hand cards, it must be put with them and another card dealt in its place, because all bets must be made on single cards.

When all the players have placed their stakes on the *réjouissance* card, the dealer must cover them with equal stakes. He then turns up the next card of the pack. If this card matches the *réjouissance* card, the dealer takes all that is staked on it. If it matches his own card, he loses all the bets on the *réjouissance* card. If this card matches neither of these nor one of the hand cards, it is placed on the table and players may bet on it also.

Another card is then dealt and the same procedure observed. As soon as the players' card is matched, the banker withdraws the pair, but he may never withdraw his own. As has been said, all cards dealt that match the hand cards must be placed with them. The deal comes to an end when a card is turned up that matches the dealer's card. When this happens, the dealer pays all outstanding stakes and passes the deal to his left. If both the hand cards are paired before the dealer's own card is matched, the dealer may, if he chooses, have a second deal.

Napoleon: This is a game that can be played by any number of players from two to six—four to six being the ideal. It is played with a full pack of fifty-two cards, which rank as in Whist (ace high). When the pack has been shuffled, the dealer (each player dealing in turn) deals out five cards to each player. The player on the left of the dealer now has the opportunity of "calling"—that is, of declaring how many tricks he thinks he can take with that hand.

He may not call one (that he will make one trick), but he may call two, three, four, or Nap five). If this player decides to pass, the player on his left has the option of the call and so on. When a call *is* made, the player on the left of the caller may, if he wishes, better that call, at which the first caller, or for that matter any of the other players, may better it further. The player who makes the highest call leads to the first trick. The first card he plays determines trumps.

The caller now plays against all the others while they try to prevent him from making the tricks he has declared to take. If the caller succeeds in his boast, he receives an arranged sum from each of the other players. Should he fail, he pays each of them this sum. If the caller makes Nap, he receives double stakes from everyone in the company.

In some circles there is a rule that when Nap has been called, the caller may draw a card from the top of the remains of the pack and either keep it or return it. If he keeps it, he discards another card from his hand.

Misère is sometimes introduced in Napoleon—that is, the caller undertakes to lose every trick. Misère is reckoned in value as three points, although it is below three in precedence of call.

Speculation: This is a game for any number of players. The full pack is used, and each player is supplied with an equal number of counters. A certain agreed number is contributed by each player to form the pool, the dealer paying double. The cards rank as is Whist (ace high). The dealer gives three cards face down to each player, and no player must look at his cards until later. Any player doing so is fined for each card looked at. These counters are put in the pool. The top card of the remainder is turned up for trumps. This extra card becomes the dealer's property, in consideration of his double payments to the pool.

The object of the game is to hold the best trump among the cards dealt. Should the turned-up card be an ace, the pool, as of right, goes to the dealer. If, otherwise, it is a fairly high one, say a ten or a court (face) card, it becomes an object of speculation, and the dealer may sell it to the highest bidder. He inquires, "Who buys?" and names his price in counters. If a purchaser is found, he pays the agreed price to the pool and places the card face up on top of his own hand.

The player on the left of the purchaser then turns up his top card, and if this is not a trump, the next player turns up a card, and so on, until a higher trump than the first should appear. When this happens, the new card, if not kept by its owner, is given to the highest bidder. If the card is not a trump, it may be beaten by the highest card that is turned up of the same suit or by another trump. This in turn becomes an object of speculation, and the owner of the highest trump exposed is exempt from turning up any other card until he has been beaten.

At the close of every round, the pool is won by the player who holds the highest card of the trump suit. If the ace of trumps is turned up, the round is concluded at once, and its owner is the winner.

This buying and selling business is often carried on to a considerable extent. Sometimes players will sell their whole hands to each other, or a single card blind on the chance of its proving a winner. Sometimes the game is played with an extra hand being dealt and placed in the middle of the table for pool. At the end of the round, this hand is examined, and if a better card is found in it than that belonging to the winner, the pool is left undisturbed and added to the next new pool. In some circles, anyone turning up a five or a jack pays one or more counters to the pool.

Pope Joan (3 or more players):   This once very popular game
is played with a pack of fifty-two cards, from which the eight
of Diamonds (for a reason which will presently appear) has
been removed, and with a special board, consisting of a
circular tray around a central pillar, divided into eight
compartments, as shown below, respectively marked Pope
(the nine of diamonds), Matrimony, Intrigue, Ace, King,
Queen, Jack, and Game. Matrimony signifies the combination in the same hand of the king and queen of the trump
suit; Intrigue that of jack and queen. The board is not

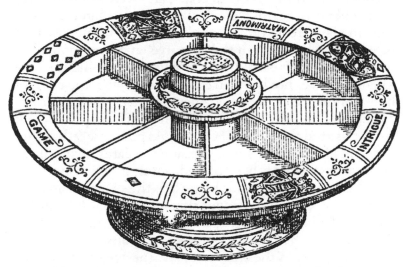

essential to the game, for a similar layout can be drawn on
paper.

Each player is provided with an equal number of
counters (say three or four dozen), each bearing an agreed
value. The first dealer then "dresses" the board—that is, he
distributes among the eight divisions fifteen counters from
his own store, as follows: six to Pope, two to Matrimony, two
to Intrigue, and one each to Ace, King, Queen, Jack, and
Game.

All the cards are then dealt out one by one but with an
extra hand being dealt to the center of the table. All players
must hold an equal number of cards, any remaining being
added to the extra hand on the table. The last card dealt
(and this will be to the extra hand) is turned up as trumps.
Should the turned-up card be Pope (nine of Diamonds), or
an ace, king, queen or jack, the dealer is entitled to all the
counters in the corresponding compartments.

The player on the dealer's left then leads any card he

pleases (ace ranking low), at the same time naming it. Let us suppose it to be the three of Diamonds. The player holding the four plays it to the three, the players holding the five, six, and seven play them in like manner. In any other suit, it would be possible to continue with the eight, but, as we have seen, the eight has been removed, thus making the seven what is called a "stop" card. That is, the run on that particular lead cannot be continued, and the player of the seven is entitled to lead next.

But besides the permanent removal of the eight of Diamonds, it will be remembered that a certain number of other (unknown) cards were dealt as an extra hand and, not being in play, create other "stop" cards. Let us suppose that the extra hand consists of the two, five, and nine of Spades, the six and ten of Hearts, the jack of Diamonds, and the king of Clubs. These, not being in circulation, make stop cards of those immediately preceding them (that is, the ace, four, and eight of Spades, the five and nine of Hearts, the ten of Diamonds, and the queen of Clubs.) As play proceeds, other cards will also become stops, because the cards next follow-ing them have already been played. Thus, in the case above, with the three of Diamonds being led, the two of Diamonds becomes a stop, and its holder should note that fact for his future guidance. All kings are necessarily stops, since they are counted as the highest cards of their suits.

Whenever, in the course of play, the ace, king, queen, or jack of the trump suit appears, the holder is entitled to all the counters in the corresponding compartment. Should king and queen, or queen and jack fall from the same hand, the holder is entitled to the proceeds of Matrimony or Intrigue, as the case may be. Anyone playing Pope takes all the counters in that division. Unless actually played, the above cards have no value, except that the player holding Pope (unplayed) is exempted from paying for any surplus cards, as will be explained.

The game proceeds as described until one of the players has played all his cards. This gives him Game and all the counters in that compartment and entitles him to receive from each other player one counter for each card such player may still hold in his hand, except for the holder of Pope, who is exempt. If Pope has been played, no exemption exists.

The skill of the player will be shown in his ability to note, on the one hand, which cards are stops, and on the other, which cards cannot be led to and should be got rid of as soon as possible. At the outset, the only *known* cards that cannot be led to are the four aces, Pope, and the next card above the turn-up (the next lower being a stop). But the list of stops increases as the game goes on. If, for instance, the nine of Hearts is known to be a stop, because the ten is in the surplus hand, it is clear that the jack cannot be led to and must itself be led in order to be got rid of.

Sequences are valuable, because they enable the player to get rid of two, three, or more cards simultaneously. Nearly as useful are alternate sequences, such as seven, nine, jack—the lowest, of course, being led. Pope, as we have seen, can only be played when its holder has the lead, and it is usually wise, therefore, to do so at the first opportunity.

The unclaimed counters in each compartment are left to accumulate. In the case of Matrimony and Intrigue, a whole evening may occasionally pass without the necessary combinations being played from the same hand, and these compartments may become very rich. The same applies to Pope, or one or more of the ace, king, queen, and jack compartments. The best method of disposing of any such counters at the close of the game is to deal a final round face up (without the surplus hand), the holder of Pope, and of the ace, king, queen, and jack of the Diamond suit being entitled to the counters in the corresponding compartments. The holder of the queen takes in addition half the amount in Matrimony and in Intrigue, the remaining halves going to the holders of the king and jack, respectively.

Newmarket (3–7 players): This is a simpler version of Pope Joan, and there is no need for the board or elaborate layout. Instead, four "luxury" cards from a spare pack are laid in a square in the center of the table: the ace of Spades, king of Hearts, queen of Clubs, and jack of Diamonds. The game is then played with a full pack from which the eight of Diamonds has been removed.

Each player stakes an agreed number of counters (preferably four or some multiple of four), and the dealer stakes double that number. The players may divide their stakes among the four luxury cards in any manner they please. The cards are then dealt out one by one to each player, with an extra hand (as in Pope Joan) to create a corresponding number of "stops." Cards left over are given to the dummy. There is no trump suit. The object of the game is for a player to exhaust his cards as quickly as possible.

The player on the dealer's left leads. He may lead any suit he pleases, but of that suit he is obliged to lead the lowest (ace, ranking low), and he names the card as he plays it. The holder of the next-highest card of the same suit plays and names it, and so on until a "stop" is reached. The player of the stop then leads to the next round. The game continues until one or other of the players is out—that is, has played all his cards. He then receives from all the other players one counter for each card left in their respective hands.

Whenever, during the course of the game, a card corresponding with one of the luxury cards is played, the player takes all the counters staked upon it. The general method of play and the division of any unclaimed stakes are the same as in the game of Pope Joan.

Spinado or *Spin* (3–7 players):   Spinado is closely related to Newmarket and is, therefore, another member of the Pope Joan family. It is played without a board and has only three pools, Matrimony, Intrigue, and Game (or First Out). To these, the dealer contributes two dozen counters—a dozen to Matrimony, half a dozen to Intrigue, and half a dozen to First Out. The other players each contribute three counters only, all of which are placed in the First Out pool.

With the four twos and the eight of Diamonds removed from the pack, the cards are dealt around, with a dummy hand as in Pope Joan. In this game there is no turn up. Matrimony is formed by the king and queen of Diamonds, Intrigue by the queen and jack of Diamonds. The ace of Diamonds is known as Spinado, or more shortly, Spin.

The player to the left of the dealer leads, and the holders of the next-highest cards in the suit play them in succession until a stop is reached, when the last player leads for a new round. The holder of Spinado, when he plays, has the option of playing it with his own card, and if he does so, he makes his card a stop. Thus, if he is playing to the six of Spades and he has the seven, he will say, "Seven and Spin." This makes the seven of Spades a stop. For this the Spinado holder receives three counters from each of the other players, and the lead passes to him.

The holder of Spinado is not bound to play it with his first card; indeed it may be to his advantage not to do so. Thus, suppose a ten of Clubs led, and the holder of Spinado has the jack and king of Clubs. It would be most unwise to play Spin with the jack, for if the jack proves to be a stop anyway, then Spin is wasted, and if any other player follows with the queen, the king (which is a stop) can follow that.

A good player, therefore, would play up to this point without declaring Spin, then play out any known stops, and finally some card which he does *not* know to be a stop together with Spin, thereby still retaining the lead. By this means he will probably be First Out and become entitled to all the counters on that pool as well as a counter for each card left in the other hands.

On the other hand, it is not safe to keep Spin back for too long, for a player holding it when one of his opponents is First Out is bound to pay the winner double—that is, two counters for every card he is left with. The holder of the king of Diamonds receives two counters from each player, when he plays it. If he plays both the king and queen of Diamonds, he also takes the Matrimony pool. Any person playing queen and jack of Diamonds takes the contents of the Intrigue pool. If the same person holds (and plays) all three cards, he takes the counters in both pools. The player of a king other than of Diamonds receives one counter from each of the other players. First Out takes the counters from that pool and is exempt from contributing to the following pool, unless, of course, he happens to be the dealer.

Slobberhannes (4 players): Why the name "Slobberhannes," no one knows. It is a game of some antiquity.

The game is played by four people with a Piquet pack of thirty-two cards (an ordinary pack from which the twos, threes, fours, fives, and sixes have been removed). The cards rank as at Whist; there are no partnerships and no trumps. The players cut for the lead, the highest card taking the lead, and the player on his right dealing. Deal and play are the same as in Whist, but the object of the game is to avoid taking the first or last trick or any trick containing the queen of Clubs. The player who wins any of these loses one point; if he wins all three, he loses a further point. One point is lost for a revoke.

The player leading has a good advantage, for he is likely to hold a safe losing card with which he will lead. The other three players will follow with the lowest card possible, except that if a player sees that he cannot avoid taking the trick, he will do so with his highest card to avoid winning a trick with it at a later stage.

The following tricks, except for the last one, may be won without damage, so long as the dreaded queen of Clubs is not among them, and the players will use these to get rid of their high cards. The great interest of this game lies in the problem of not being left with the queen of Clubs, and it will soon be appreciated that the holders of the ace and king of Clubs are in a very dangerous position until the queen is out of the way. These three cards, therefore, are discarded as soon as possible. The best card of any suit of which there are only a few remaining is a very bad card to lead; besides being certain of winning, it offers the opponents an opportunity to discard one or more of the three highest Clubs.

Sift Smoke (2–8 players):   A complete pack of cards is divided into two halves, one portion being dealt to the players and the other remaining in the center of the table. The player receiving the last card of the deal names its suit as trumps. The cards rank as at Whist. The tricks are of no value, but each player must follow the suit led or play a trump. For each trick gained, the player takes a card from the undealt portion and adds it to his hand, and he who can hold out the longest wins the round.

Catch the Ten, or *Scotch Whist:*   This game may be played by any number from two to eight. The pack used consists of thirty-six cards, the twos, threes, fours, and fives being removed. It is important that the cards should be dealt around equally. To ensure this, if there are five or seven players, one of the sixes is also removed. With eight, all the sixes are removed—that is, the game is played with the thirty-two card Piquet pack.

If the party consists of two, three, five, or seven, each plays on his own account. Four play in partnership, as at Whist. Six players may either play three against three, or in three couples, each couple playing against the two others. Eight may play either four against four or in four independent partnerships, each pair against the other three. Partners and adversaries sit alternately.

Even where only two play, the cards are so dealt as to give three separate hands to each, all of which are played independently. In like manner, if three play, two hands are dealt to each. Dealing is by one card at a time, the last card being turned up by way of trump.

The cards, other than trumps, rank as at Whist. In the

trump suit the jack takes precedence, the order being jack, ace, king, queen, ten, nine, eight, seven, six.

Game is forty-one points. The object of the game is to secure the tricks containing certain cards, which have a special scoring value as follows:

Jack of trumps .... 11 points
Ten of trumps .... 10 points
Ace of trumps .... 4 points
King of trumps .... 3 points
Queen of trumps .... 2 points

In addition to these, the players score for "cards"—that is, for all cards they take in excess of their numerical proportion of the pack. Thus, if four are playing, their quota would be nine cards each. If the players on one side secure seven tricks (28 cards), they are ten in excess of their quota and score ten accordingly for cards.

The play follows the rules of ordinary Whist, but the special object of the game is to "catch the ten," as it makes practically a difference of twenty to the score. The jack is an even better card, but, being the leading trump, it necessarily remains with the side who received it by the deal.

Thirty-One (the German *Schnautz*): This is a simple and lively card game for any number of persons. The full pack is used, and the cards rank as at Whist.

The players, having put an agreed stake in the pool, each receive three cards dealt face down. Three additional cards are dealt face up in the middle of the table. The players, beginning with the elder hand, draw one card each from the hand in the middle of the table, replacing it with a discard from their own hand, which is also left face up.

The primary object of the game is to hold three cards of the same suit, which, added together, make thirty-one—the ace counting eleven, court cards ten each, and the other cards according to their nominal value. Obviously the desired number can only be made by an ace and two "ten" cards. Next in scoring value to thirty-one is a triplet— between two or more triplets, the higher has preference. Triplets count thirty and a half, and therefore override thirty. In default of thirty-one or a triplet, the highest total *in one suit* wins.

The discarding process continues until either one of the

party makes thirty-one, in which case he shows his cards and claims the pool, or until some other player signifies by a knock on the table that he is content (with his hand, that is). Should this occur, each of the other players (but not the one who knocked), has a right to exchange one more card, after which the hands are shown, and the highest takes the pool.

5

Marbles

here are many versions of this very old game, and the mastery of all of them depends on the skill of shooting the marble. No rules exist as to how the marble should be propelled, but the only accurate way of doing so is known as fulking. The marble to be shot is placed just above the joint of the thumb of the right hand and held there by the tip of the forefinger, the top of the thumb being firmly grasped by the middle finger. Aim is then taken and the thumb let fly with enough force as to shoot the marble with the required speed. With practice, sufficient skill may be obtained to hit another marble at several feet distance. In discharging the marble, great care should be taken to keep the hand perfectly still. The forefinger should rest on the floor.

As the majority of marble games need a good stretch of space free from obstacles, I give here three versions that are suitable for playing indoors.

Bridge-Board or *Arch-Board:*   For this game a narrow piece of cardboard, about 14 by 1½ inches, is required. In this, nine arches are cut, each being about an inch in height and about three quarters of an inch wide. Another piece of cardboard or a piece of wood should be attached to the back of the strip to make it stand up. Over each arch a number is written, these numbers being at the discretion of the players, but no number over eight is allowed. The lower numbers should be in the middle of the bridge and the higher ones at the two sides. A good arrangement for beginners is 3 3 2 1 0 1 2 3 3.

One player is made the first bridge keeper, and the rest shoot their marbles from a line about four feet from the bridge. Every marble that fails to go through a hole is paid to the bridge keeper, but for every successful shot the bridge keeper pays the corresponding number of marbles to the shooter. As the position of bridge keeper is usually a lucrative one, it is best changed at every round.

Bounce Eye: A circle, about a foot in diameter, is drawn on the ground; in a carpeted room, a circular piece of paper of the same size may be used. Each player contributes one marble toward the pool, and these marbles are formed into a group in the middle of the circle. The players then take it in turns to stand over the ring, and after taking aim, let a marble fall into the pool.

Expert fulkers will use that method of propelling the marble in order to give its fall more force. If, as a result of the latter operation, any marbles are driven out of the circle, they are taken up by the player. If no marbles are driven out, the aimed marble becomes part of the pool, which is then re-formed in the middle of the ring.

Knock-Out or *Lag-Out:*   Any number of players may join in this game. From a line about six feet from the wall, each player in turn fulks a marble against the wall so that it rebounds. When a marble on the rebound strikes some other marble, *all* the marbles on the floor become the property of the successful thrower. Any marble that rebounds beyond the throwing line is placed halfway between the throwing line and the wall.

Hairry My Bossie: This is a game of chance for two players. One player puts a number of marbles (from one to five) into the hollow of his closed hand and says, "How many?" In some parts of the country the phrase, "Hairry my bossie" (hairry = rob; bossie = wooden bowl) is used. The other answers, "Knock him down," upon which the player holding the marbles puts closed hands on his knees and continues to strike them up and down on his knee in order to give his opponent some idea of the number.

   He then says, "How many blows?" and gets the reply "As many as goes." A guess is then made. If the guess is correct, the guesser wins the marbles. If it is incorrect, the guesser has to make up the difference between the number guessed and the real number. The players play alternately.

6

Forfeits

Strictly speaking, any player found guilty of a misdemeanor during the course of a parlor game should, as a punishment, give up to the forfeit master one of his or her personal belongings—a key, a handkerchief, a coin, a brooch, etc. Then, toward the end of the proceedings, the forfeit master should hold up these objects one by one, saying the following couplet:

"I have a thing and a very pretty thing,
And who is the owner of this very pretty thing?"

The owner of the object, in order to regain his possession, claims it and in return is compelled to perform a task, either ridiculous or seemingly impossible (or both), although sometimes it may be tolerably pleasant. There follows a selection from the hundreds of different "forfeits" exacted by Victorian forfeit masters.

In a large party the business of confiscating and then redeeming personal objects may be too lengthy, and in such circumstances a selection of the following forfeits could be written on separate slips of paper and each enclosed in an envelope. As each penalty is earned, the name of the defaulter is inscribed on an envelope. Some of the punishments take only a few seconds to inflict. Others are as long and involved as the games that produced them, and they may even involve the awarding of further forfeits.

The time to be allowed at the end of the party for the playing out of the forfeits should be kept in mind when the selection of them is being made. If some of the more involved and amusing forfeits are to be enacted, it is a good idea to restrict the awarding of penalties to only a few of the games.

GENERAL FORFEITS

The Deaf Man: The individual who is punished with deafness is made to stand in the middle of the room and to answer three questions with the words, "I'm deaf; I can't hear." The fourth time he is addressed, however, he must say, "I can hear," and must do whatever is asked of him.

The fun, to all but the penitent, is to make the first three proposals agreeable ones—such as bringing him a lady to kiss, to which command, of course, he must turn his deaf ear. The second offer might be that of a sum of money, which again he cannot hear. The fourth communication is, of course, an unpleasant one for him. He may be asked to take the same lady to be kissed by another gentleman, to sing a comic song, perform a dance, etc. This fourth command he must obey.

The Dummy: This consists in executing all acts of penitence ordered by other members of the party without uttering a word.

To Perform the Parrot: The penitent taking the part of the parrot must approach each person in the company, or, if there are too many present, any specified number. He or she must ask, "If I were a parrot, what would you have me say?" and must then repeat the answer in a parrot voice. If the parrot is a lady, one gentleman—but one only—may have her say, "Kiss your pretty Poll," and pretty Poll must say this and then submit to her own request.

Three Questions: The victim must leave the room while three questions are devised, to which he must answer either "yes" or "no" without knowing what they are until *after* he has answered them.

Show the Spirit of Contrary: Whatever the player is told to do, he must do just the opposite.

The Living Statue: The victim must stand on a chair or stool and adopt the pose of any personality the others choose.

Make a Perfect Woman: This forfeit is a charming one. The player must select from the ladies present the personal features or traits that he most admires in each. In this way he has the opportunity of paying compliments to all the ladies, although, of course, the task requires great tact.

Give Good Advice: The player gives every member of the company what he considers to be a piece of good advice.

Make Your Will: The victim goes from player to player telling each one what he will receive as a legacy. To a bald man he may leave his hair, to another his common sense, to another his good looks, etc.

Blind Man's Waltz: A forfeit to punish a lady and a gentleman. They are both blindfolded and must waltz together.

The Cordial Greeting: A double forfeit. Two players are blindfolded and placed in opposite corners of the room. They must then find each other and, if a lady and a gentleman, must kiss. If two gentlemen, they must approach one another, arms outstretched, meet and shake hands.

Ennui: The player must yawn until he makes someone else yawn.

Nose and Ears: The wrongdoer is required to grasp his left ear with his right hand and his nose with his left hand. He must then uncross his hands, slap his knees and reverse his original position—that is, grasp his right ear with his left hand and his nose with his right. This must be done *rapidly* many times in succession. Unless he is an accomplished artist at this movement, the player will do little more than make gestures that promote much mirth.

Stiff as a Stake: The penitent must lie full length on the floor and cry in imploring tones, "Here I lie, stiff as a stake, who'll come and save me, for pity's sake!" To release a lady, a gentleman must kiss her and help her to her feet. To release a gentleman, one of the ladies must pull his hair and try to prevent him from rising.

Kiss Your Own Shadow: A gentleman thus condemned has

a cunning way out. He arranges for his shadow to fall on the face of a lady and *then* he kisses it.

Blind Dancers: If the end of a party is near and there are still many forfeits to be redeemed, those left to do penance may all be blindfolded and compelled to go through the motions of whatever is the popular dance of the day. This collective punishment (which sometimes threatens to become a massacre) makes a good finale to any party.

SHORT AND TRICK FORFEITS

Call Your Sweetheart's Name up the Chimney

Laugh in One Corner of the Room, Cry in Another, Sing in Another, and Dance in Another

Put Four Chairs in a Row, Take off Your Shoes, and Jump over Them: Even young ladies can perform this feat, for it is the shoes over which they jump.

Ask a Question to Which the Answer Cannot Possibly Be "no":   The question is, "What does Y-E-S spell?"

Bite an Inch off a Hot Poker (or any other similar object):   The secret is to hold the poker about an inch *off* the face and then to take an imaginary bite.

Lie Down on the Floor and Rise with Your Arms Folded

Put Yourself Through the Keyhole: The word "yourself" should be written on a piece of paper and put through the keyhole.

Kiss a Book Inside and Outside Without Opening It: The book may be kissed inside the room and outside it.

Place a Book on the Floor So That No One Can Jump Over It: The book is placed next to the wall.

Put One Hand Where the Other Cannot Touch It: On the elbow.

Constantinople: This absurd trick is included here because it was once the most popular of all forfeits. It was made even more absurd because everyone knew what was coming. The condemned player had to spell out the word "Constantinople," as follows: "C-o-n, Con; s-t-a-n, stan; t-i, ti," at which point the rest of the players shouted, "No, no!" implying that the victim had made a mistake.

Being Friendly: The player in default must walk around the room and bestow a friendly smile on every other person in turn.

KISSING FORFEITS

Opportunity (a double forfeit for a lady and gentleman):   The couple must go into a corner of the room and spell aloud together the word "Opportunity." If, in ignorance of the joke, the couple do not kiss while they have the opportunity *instead* of spelling the word, there is much laughter at their expense, and they are rewarded with a further punishment. This, of course, should be another kissing forfeit.

The Beggar: This is an unusual punishment in that its ending is a happy one for the wrongdoer. The penitent approaches a lady and falls on his knees before her, imploring charity. She, touched by his distress, asks him: "Do you want bread?" "Do you want water?" "Do you want a penny?" etc. To all these questions the beggar shakes his head impatiently. At length the lady must say "Do you want a kiss?" At this the beggar jumps up and accepts the offer.

The Sulks: This is a punishment awarded to ladies only. The lady paying the forfeit is ordered to sulk. This she does after whispering into the ear of the forfeit master the name of a gentleman on whom she would like to bestow a kiss. The forfeit master then presents the gentlemen to her one by one, making sure that the one of her choice is well at the back of the line. As they are presented, the lady turns her back on them all, in a sulky, pouting manner, until the arrival of the fortunate one of her choice to whom she offers, and from whom she receives, a kiss.

Languishing: This is another forfeit in which the wrongdoer comes off best, and the punishment descends on an innocent. The penitent is ordered into a corner to languish. This he does by simply going there and saying, "I languish." He is then asked, "For whom do you languish?" and he answers by naming any player of the opposite sex to come and kiss him.

The lady then languishes for a gentleman, who approaches her, kisses her, and languishes for another lady, and so on until all the players have been called from their places, and form a line of ladies and gentlemen placed alternately. When the line is complete, the original languisher turns around and walks along the line kissing all the ladies. The lady left at the top does the same to all the gentlemen—and so on, down to the last player, who, having no one to kiss, has every reason to languish.

To Make a Wallflower of Oneself: If a lady is to pay the forfeit, she must place herself with her back to the wall until she has been kissed twice, by two different gentlemen, each of whom she must herself ask to come and kiss her. If this forfeit falls upon a gentleman, he must place himself against the wall until any *one* lady takes compassion on him, and releases him with a kiss.

The Candelabra: This is a forfeit for gentlemen only. The miscreant, known as the Candelabra, must give a handkerchief to another. Then, taking a light in his own hand, he must conduct the other gentleman to a lady. The handkerchief holder kisses the lady but the poor Candelabra must not; he only has his lips wiped with his own handkerchief by his companion. They then proceed to the next lady, and so on around the room.

To Fish for a Kiss: This is a forfeit for ladies only. A grape or plum or the like is tied to a piece of thread and suspended from a pen or pencil to resemble a fishing rod. Any gentleman then approaches the lady and dangles the bait near her lips. She is compelled under the terms of the forfeit to take the bait in her teeth and must not let it go.

Having thus hooked his fish, the angler then leads her around the room saying, "See what a fine fish I have hooked!" He then detaches the rod, and taking the line up into his own mouth, he gradually approaches the lady until, inevitably, their lips meet. At this he gives her a kiss.

Three Kissing Questions: The forfeiter is sent out of the room while the remainder of the company try to devise three questions that will ensure some kissing by their answers. The forfeit holder must answer "yes" or "no" to these questions *before* knowing what they are. The questions might be these:

1.   Would you like to be kissed by every gentleman (or lady) in the room?
2.   Would you like (so-and-so) *not* to kiss you?
3.   Would you like (so-and-so) to kiss you?

To Run the Gauntlet: This is for a lady. The gentlemen range themselves in two lines to form an avenue. One of them then conducts the lady to the first gentleman, who demands a kiss as price of passage; the avenue being thus opened, each gentleman tries to obtain a kiss before letting the lady pass, but he must not step out of his place to get it. He may only stop her with his hands, but she may use any pretense she chooses, and also try to push her way through in order to pass without any kisses at all, or with only those she chooses to receive. If a gentleman moves out of his place to obtain a kiss, he, as a punishment, is condemned to stand in the middle of the room, with a lighted candle in each hand, until a lady releases him by kissing him.

To Give a Kiss à la Capuchin: This is a double forfeit for a lady and a gentleman. The lady and gentleman kneel back to back and mutually try to kiss each other by turning their heads.

To Choose from Three Actions: For a gentleman. A lady, whose identity is unknown to the wrongdoer, makes three gestures behind his back. A tap on the chin, a box on the ear, and a kiss. He does not know in which order the gestures are made but must choose "first, second, or third." Whichever he chooses he gets!

The Sofa: The penitent, on all fours, resembles a sofa, upon which a lady and a gentleman sit comfortably and exchange a kiss.

The Rabbit's Kiss: A double forfeit for a lady and gentleman. The couple kneel at a short distance from each other, holding the ends of about a yard of thread in their mouths. At a given signal they diminish the distance between them by drawing the thread into their mouths until their lips meet in a kiss.

Kissing a Nun: A double forfeit for a lady and gentleman. The couple kiss through the bars of the back of a chair.

The Pilgrim: A gentleman conducts a lady around the room, saying to all the other gentlemen, "A kiss for my sister, a morsel of bread for me." To the ladies he says, "A morsel of bread for my sister and a kiss for me." The bread is of no importance, but the kisses are indispensable.

The Clock: The guilty party, the clock, stands before the mantel and calls a player of the opposite sex. The person called asks the clock what time it is. The clock replies whatever hour he or she likes and receives the same number of kisses.

The Hobby Horse or *Ariadne's Leopard:*   The penitent, on his hands and knees, is obliged to carry around the room, seated on his back, a lady whom all the gentlemen (the penitent excepted) are privileged to kiss in turn.

The Kiss of Chance: The owner of the forfeit takes the four kings and the four queens from a pack of cards, shuffles them, and deals them to four ladies and four gentlemen. Whoever has the king of Hearts kisses the one who has the queen of Hearts and so on. He who has dealt merely watches. This is his punishment.

I'm in a Well: The victim must stand with his back to the wall, then choose a partner who stands facing him. This partner then chooses another partner of the opposite sex to stand with his back to her, and so on until all the company are standing in pairs in this way.

On choosing his partner, the victim must say, "I'm in a well," to which someone must ask, "How many feet deep?" The answer may be any number up to ten. He is then asked, "Whom will you have to pull out?" and the one named stands next to him.

When all have chosen a partner and are in position,

each couple turns around so that No. 2 faces No. 3, No. 4 faces No. 5, and so on, leaving No. 1 facing the wall. Then all the couples kiss each other as many times as the gentleman was feet in the well, but poor No. 1 is left to kiss the wall.

Second-Hand Kisses: This penalty is inflicted upon a lady. She who is to be punished chooses a female friend. This friend then presents herself to a gentleman who kisses her, and she then has to carry the kiss back to her companion. This performance is repeated as many times as there are gentlemen in the company.

Kiss the Lady You Love Without Anyone's Knowing It: If the victim is in the know, he will kiss *all* the ladies in the room, including, of course, the one he most admires.

Kneel to the Wittiest, Bow to the Prettiest, and Kiss the One You Love: They must *not* be one and the same, and this makes the task fraught with perils.

Postman's Knock: This is a game in its own right, which is often used as a forfeit. The instructions for play are on p. 52.

Index of Games

141